+ReCharge!

Boost your resilience in a crazy, post-pandemic world

Tim Farish & **Matthew Gregory**

Book design by: Steve Kelly (MFS) www.ikelly.co.uk
Cover image & Typesetting by: SWATT Books Ltd www.swatt-books.co.uk

Printed in the United Kingdom
First Printing, 2021

ISBN: 978-1-8383437-0-5 (Paperback)
ISBN: 978-1-8383437-1-2 (eBook)

Recharge! Publishing
Bartons Byre, Worcester Road
Hagley, Stourbridge
West Midlands   DY9 OPR

www.rechargeability.com

THE ENERGY OF THE MIND IS THE ESSENCE OF LIFE.

ARISTOTLE,
THE PHILOSOPHY OF ARISTOTLE

MIND  ·······>

BODY  ·······>

EMOTION  ·······>

Focus

How to focus
Managing distractions & flow
Attention training

page 11

Agility

Power of choice
Growth mindset
Managing attachments

page 29

Boundaries

Valuing self
Managing boundaries
Courageous conversations

page 49

Restore

Sleep management
Relaxation strategies
'Off' button

page 65

Refuel

Energy diet
Exercise
Movement

page 79

Enjoy

Finding joy
Develop learning openness
Sharing

page 93

Meaning

Living with purpose
Gratitude & appreciation
Develop your intuition

page 105

Mood

Managing self-talk
Managing emotions
Managing mood

page 115

Connect

Meaningful relationships
Kindness & compassion
Connection to nature

page 131

Why Recharge?

The simple fact is that exhaustion and stress have become an epidemic that companies cannot ignore.

One of the biggest challenges we face as individuals is how we manage our energy.

Too many of us limp into the weekend in a state of exhaustion and relief. And if we put family demands into the equation, then that relief doesn't last long. The pace of working life has been increasing for some time and we have lost since the advent of social media – and with it, the always-on culture of 24/7 availability – the protection that pre-digital boundaries offered.

Now, with the onset of homeworking due to Covid-19, the boundaries between work and home life have become even more blurred. The simple fact is that exhaustion and stress have become an epidemic that companies cannot ignore. And the cost does not just stop with organizations. If our energy reserves are low, we are seriously reduced in our capacity to love and be present at home, so our family life suffers too. The two are inseparable.

The last few years have seen an increase in the demands and drains on resilience in the workplace, yet corporate wellbeing programmes are often woefully inadequate in addressing the problem, as it is so deep and pervasive. It's not that the help offered is wrong – far from it – it's just that it often is not holistic enough to address the challenge properly. And that challenge is very clear.

There is an energy deficit which leads to exhaustion, burnout and depression. In other words, too many of us are running on empty for too long. And our numbers are growing frighteningly quickly.

"Too many of us are running on empty for too long. And our numbers are growing frighteningly quickly."

+ReCharge!

This book has been designed to help with this problem. While relatively simple in design, the RECHARGE! model is designed to be a potent and holistic personal development tool in its own right, as well as providing a powerful approach to looking after yourself and recharging your batteries.

A lot of thinking about building resilience is defensive – how do I react when I'm on my knees or coping with a tragic, often unexpected, event? The RECHARGE! model can certainly help here – we know it from our own personal experience. However, resilience is not only about just dealing with extremes - we believe it is about having a consistent strategy of looking after yourself on a day-to-day basis. The RECHARGE! model is one that is based on flourishing; it is proactive and preventative as well as defensive and reactive.

We have used a battery metaphor because our mobile phones, which run on batteries, get depleted by use, and if we don't recharge them overnight, we start getting low battery alerts. If we ignore them, an impressively powerful bit of kit stops functioning altogether. Humans are like that too. If you keep taking and don't recharge, you will get plenty of warning signs, and if you ignore them, your quality of functioning will diminish and eventually stop! Sound dramatic? Check out the story of António Horta-Osório, Group Chief Executive, Lloyds Banking Group[1] who ended up spending nine days in the Priory clinic, dosed up on sleeping pills and resting 16 hours a day to stave off total nervous breakdown. He didn't recharge and paid a high price for this.

Thankfully, looking after ourselves has become more acceptable - particularly with the challenges we've all had to face through the pandemic - and we hope our approach can give you the skills and confidence to flourish.

The RECHARGE! model is one that is based on flourishing; it is proactive and preventative.

"If you keep taking and don't recharge you will get plenty of warning signs."

Why Recharge?

By taking our RECHARGE! test before you start, you can see for yourself where best to focus.

Scan the code to take our recharge diagnostic test now

"So be guided by our diagnostic... if you're exhausted and not sleeping properly... get on with that."

Sadly, many people, faced by the overwhelming pressures of life, are more concerned about recharging their smartphone each night than recharging themselves. And it shows! We all carry a level of resilience charge, and when you meet people, you instinctively get a sense of their charge levels. We are generally not drawn to people who are running on empty. Recharging, as well as being concerned with our sense of wellbeing, also affects how vibrant and influential we are.

You will most likely already have some recharge practices, or else you wouldn't be reading this book. But our experience of working with thousands of leaders and professionals is that you will benefit from strengthening these practices – for all the reasons mentioned earlier.

This book, based on comprehensive research, will show you how. In fact, EVERY part of the RECHARGE! Model is present because of solid evidence that backs up how it can support both your flourishing and replenish your resilience charge. We cite our research throughout as well as supporting it with stories and examples.

Furthermore, we have both lived and experienced this model through considerable personal challenges - including tragedy - and it has helped us flourish and maintain balance through the most brutal situations that life can throw at you.

With this in mind, the content in this book has been put together in a sequential order of sections which build on each other. However, the order presented might not correspond to the area of recharging you actually need to focus on first. So, be guided by our diagnostic.

+ReCharge!

By taking our RECHARGE! test before you start, you can see for yourself where best to focus your attention in the areas which most need it first. If you're exhausted and not sleeping properly, for instance, then it's best to get on with that before you start to build your charge in other parts of the model.

So feel free to start where you need to, and trust that you can come back to the other areas when you are ready. Being a holistic model – all areas are connected in some way – trust that with improvements in one area, you will also be making a positive impact in others.

At the end of the book, we've also added a section for people that lead teams – How Leaders Can Build the Resilience of Their Teams – to round everything off.

The principles in this book are even more essential now that we live in a world where the illusion of certainty, particularly in material things, is something we would be wise to accept. Economies come and go, as does our wealth and the world order, yet human, universal truths don't. And truth #1 is that we need to look inside ourselves a little more than we thought, to maximize our life energy.

Wiser heads than ours have known this for thousands of years. In fact, the essence of this book is ancient, in wisdom terms, in helping people identify a more holistic, less materialistic way of life. This, we believe, gives us energy, meaning and hope.

Tim & Matt

Improvements in one area WILL make a positive impact in others.

"We need to look inside ourselves a little more than we thought."

Mind

How to focus
Managing distractions & flow
Attention training

Focus

Power of choice
Growth mindset
Managing attachments

Agility

Valuing self
Managing boundaries
Courageous conversations

Boundaries

FOCUS

HOW TO FOCUS

·

MANAGING DISTRACTION & FLOW

·

ATTENTION TRAINING

How to focus

> "Energy is the essence of life. Every day you decide how you're going to use it by knowing what you want and what it takes to reach that goal, and by maintaining focus."

Oprah Winfrey *

Where can we start a book about Recharging and managing your resilience?

At the beginning. Because if you cannot focus properly, it's unlikely that you'll change, improve yourself or achieve anything worthwhile. And the reason you're reading this is because you're interested in improving something very important – how you look after your mental, physical and emotional wellbeing, and how you manage your energy better.

The good news is that this book gives you the areas we believe you need to focus on in order to do that. But you still need to make it a priority and give it a go. In other words, you will need to focus properly and lend it your attention.

+ReCharge!

How to focus

To help, let's start by demystifying what we mean by focus.

Focus is the ability to know how you want to spend your time and energy. It has two components: Choosing WHAT to spend your time on and choosing your ATTITUDE as you execute those choices.

To help develop this even further we'll introduce you to the concept of growth mindsets (see AGILITY section) in the next chapter.

But for now - here's an example. You've got to do a presentation. You need to find your focus. You do not want to have an attitude that you will hate it and the audience might be bored; instead you choose to focus your energy on learning something and believing that you might even enjoy it. In other words, by treating a challenge as an opportunity for growth and learning you are consciously developing a growth mindset. And the pay-off is a huge boost to your energy.

A truism about focus is that what you place your attention on grows in importance and starts to dominate your time. Additionally, the more you choose how you want to do something, the more energized you will feel.

"Instead of focusing on the circumstances that you cannot change – focus strongly and powerfully on the circumstances that you can."

Joy Page

How to focus

> "My success, part of it certainly, is that I have focused in on a few things."

Bill Gates

So where does it sometimes go wrong?

The focus for most of us is pretty straightforward: our jobs, our roles (e.g. parents, child, friend) and the interests we have developed. As the years go by, we've learnt to build our lives around these aspects. This means there are two issues which can interfere with our energy levels:

Issue one is when we start to focus too much on other people's demands; it is then that these obligations start to dominate our lives and our sense of control starts to fade. This means that over time we lose our energy and, in turn, our motivation, and we start to slip into survival mode. It's almost as if our agenda gradually got lost and we forgot we even used to have one. We call this the box of 'Deception' in our mapping exercise at the end of this section.

Issue two can arise when we have too many things we are focused on, so that in fact we lack focus. Our to-do list grows and with it our sense of being overwhelmed, and both these factors seem to feed off each other. In our experience, nobody ever suffers when they reduce their to-do list, although it can be a difficult and demanding process because of Issue 1 above. In fact, the opposite happens – productivity is often unleashed.

This is why it's really important to have a strategy to deal with distractions, as they will inevitably derail you unless you get brutal with them. And we have included an exercise to help you with this.

+ReCharge!

So, now we have defined how FOCUS works, let's get practical and start working on it.

Here are some different ways to explore the topic of focus:

- For those who feel that life has lost its purpose, now is a good time to consider reading the EMOTION – MEANING section of this book to give you some inspiration. You can then come back here to do the rest of the exercises.

- For those who simply want to focus better and gain more energy, the following reflections and exercises will help. The first exercise is a two-part mapping designed to improve what you focus on. This is then followed by exercises on MANAGING DISTRACTIONS AND FINDING FLOW and ATTENTION TRAINING.

Before we can work on improving our focus, it's important to get a reality check on how we actually use our time and expend our energy. The first exercise will map out your current reality and the following one will prompt you to make different choices to improve and increase your energy levels.

"Lack of direction, not lack of time, is the problem. We all have twenty-four hour days."

Zig Ziglar

How to focus

> "Tell me what you are committed to, and I'll tell you what you will be in 20 years. We become whatever we are committed to."
>
> **Rick Warren**

Instructions

The time-energy matrix on page 18 maps out how we typically use our time and in turn, our energy in quadrants. The colour boxes refer to the areas that drain our energy in order of severity (RED, ORANGE and YELLOW) and those that recharge us (GREEN).

The two variables for how we measure this are by 'Urgency' and 'Importance' and you will see this represented in the quadrants.

Urgent activities demand immediate attention and are often associated with the achievement of someone else's goals. They also have immediate consequences if they are not treated as high priority.

Important activities help you achieve your personal and professional goals and often demand concentrated efforts over a longer time period. They typically have long-term and often not immediate consequences.

All four quadrants come with a description, for instance 'Derailers', which aptly captures their essence. Each quadrant has value, for example there is genuine enjoyment and some value in 'Escape' but we need to limit it if we want to maximise our energy. Likewise, 'Derailers' are necessary if we work in teams and want to invest in others but again, we need to manage this.

+ReCharge!

The first matrix on page 19 gives you examples of the typical activities within each quadrant and the next matrix is for you to fill in, mapping out the reality of these activities during a time period lasting, for instance, for 30 days. The final matrix on page 21 is designed to give you an opportunity to design how you like to use your time and energy going forward and starts putting you more in control.

Please consider the percentage of time (%) you typically spend in each box and give it a figure in the brackets. This will provide an idea of your stress levels (RED, ORANGE, YELLOW) and what you need to focus on and change to improve your energy. To help with this, there are reflective exercises included to guide you. Our suggestion is to choose a month but you can choose a time period that works for your life, e.g. a typical week, month or quarter judging on the intensity of activities.

> "The more you deny reality, the crueller reality is to you."
>
> **Cary Nieuwhof**

How to focus

#1

URGENT – IMPORTANT
'PROBLEM SOLVING'

Deadlines
Crisis
Pressing issues
Client/Key stakeholder problems
Medical emergencies

#2

NOT URGENT – IMPORTANT
'LEADERSHIP/MASTERY'

Relationship building
Strategic visioning
Goal planning
Personal development
Business development
Strategic networking
Problem solving
Investing in others
Exercise and recreation
Time with family and friends
Essential admin

#3

URGENT – NOT IMPORTANT
'DERAILERS'

Low priority email
Most social media
Some phone calls
Some meetings
Low priority demands
Most interruptions

#4

NOT URGENT – NOT IMPORTANT
'ESCAPE'

Extensive web surfing/tv viewing
Extensive gaming
Time-wasters
Habitual workplace gossip
Indulgent social planning
Blaming, moaning, whining

+ReCharge!

#1

URGENT – IMPORTANT (%)
'PROBLEM SOLVING'

#2

NOT URGENT – IMPORTANT (%)
'LEADERSHIP/MASTERY'

#3

URGENT – NOT IMPORTANT (%)
'DERAILERS'

#4

NOT URGENT – NOT IMPORTANT (%)
'ESCAPE'

How to focus

Post-exercise reflections

What is the % total of RED, ORANGE, YELLOW that drains your energy?

What is the % of GREEN that helps recharge your energy?

What's the difference % (+/-)?

RED

How you can 'manage' these better the next time they arise? For example, a significant chunk of time spent on activities in this quadrant, comes from requests from others. Do you need to say 'no' more? DO you need to push-back on unreasonable requests caused by someone else's poor planning. If this resonates as true **consider reading the EMOTION – BOUNDARIES section of this book which looks at how to set and enforce boundaries.**

What practical improvements can help you deal with these activities to make them less stressful?

ORANGE

How can you 'avoid' these better when they arise?

What can you reduce by delegation or push back on?

YELLOW

How can you 'limit' these better when they arise?

What can you cut out and stop?

GREEN

How can you 'focus' more on these?

What can you practically do to protect these activities in your calendar?

+ReCharge!

The final mapping exercise below looks at how you ideally want to spend your time and energy for the next month.

Time in RED is inevitable and can even be enjoyable, but unless you reduce your time in ORANGE and YELLOW, you will start to burn out. The important thing is to consciously spend as much % time as possible on your agenda (GREEN), as this will give you energy and provide a balance in your life. In order to do that, you will need to have strategies to 'manage' RED, 'avoid' ORANGE and 'limit' YELLOW effectively. The reflections you've made above should give you some ideas as to how you can do this.

#1

URGENT – IMPORTANT (%)
'PROBLEM SOLVING'

#2

NOT URGENT – IMPORTANT (%)
'LEADERSHIP/MASTERY'

#3

URGENT – NOT IMPORTANT (%)
'DERAILERS'

#4

NOT URGENT – NOT IMPORTANT (%)
'ESCAPE'

"Focus is a matter of deciding what things you're not going to do."

John Carmack

Managing distractions and finding flow

> "Flow is a source of mental energy in that it focuses attention and motivates action."
>
> **Mihaly Csikszentmihalyi**

What is 'flow'?

Psychologist Mihaly Csikszentmihalyi studied more than 1,000 people to learn what makes them happy. He found that people feel happiest when they focus on a single activity that challenges them but is not too difficult, includes a well-defined objective and provides quick feedback. When people engage in such activities, they don't feel the passing of time anymore; they are "in the flow."

It's a state of almost unconscious action, where the body (rather than the conscious brain) runs the show. Actions are effortless, more fluid and natural, unlike the clumsy interventions of the under-evolved conscious part of our 'intellectual' brain (unconscious competence versus conscious competence).

"One look at an email can rob you of 15 minutes of focus. One call on your cell phone, one tweet, one instant message can destroy your schedule, forcing you to move meetings, or blow off really important things, like love, and friendship."

Jacqueline Leo

+ReCharge!

So here are your training exercises, first to Manage distractions and finding flow, then Attention training.

Managing distraction and finding flow – Application activity

1. Identify something important and challenging that you need to progress (for example something in your green boxes), e.g. 'Write proposal for client A' or 'Scope out project B'

2. Block out some time in your calendar to work on it

3. Book a space where you can work uninterrupted

4. Consider if there is any preparation you need to do beforehand, e.g. information you'll need, or input from others that will be helpful

5. Beforehand, ideally at least 48 hours, start creating a plan for how you'll use the time. Identify the steps you'll take and maybe the high-level sequence of tasks

6. Once in that space, turn off all digital notifications, e.g. put your phone on silent, put your email out of office on. What else could distract you? Have a plan for dealing with it, e.g. having a note pad to capture ideas, concerns or things to do that are unrelated to the task in hand

7. Write down your ideal outcome from this time, e.g. 'I will have a draft proposal for client A that I feel proud of', or 'I will have an initial scope for project B that feels well thought through and gives me confidence'

8. Start working on the task

   a. Notice when it starts to feel difficult and you want to distract yourself with something easier. Stay with it. Take a break, have a walk, but stay with the task

9. Once your time is up, take 5 minutes to answer these questions:

   a. How satisfied do you feel with the outputs? (1 = low; 10 = high)

   b. When did you hit 'flow' (absorbed and losing track of time)?

   c. How energised do you feel about the task you worked on? (1 = low; 10 = high)

Attention training

> "Our study shows that mindfulness training and sustained practice produces statistically significant improvement in three capabilities that are important for successful leadership in the 21st century: resilience, the capacity for collaboration, and the ability to lead in complex conditions."
>
> **Megan Reitz and Michael Chaskalson**
> **HBR, 4 Nov 2016**

"That meditation works is no longer in doubt; modern science has proved it lowers stress and anxiety by measurable amounts, and can reduce irritability and frustration, while increasing compassion and empathy."

Rachel Carlyle [4]

Ever been in a meeting and your mind keeps wandering to an incident that happened in the previous meeting?

Ever been in a meeting and your mind keeps wandering to the next meeting you're about to attend?

Ever been working on something that requires some serious thought and your mind keeps wandering to something else?

Me too! And when I worked at KPMG Corporate Finance, it was a big issue for senior people there.

According to Amishi Jha, a neuroscientist specializing in the brain mechanisms of attention[2], this **mental time-travel (chewing over the past, speculating about the future), if unmanaged, can affect the quality of our decision-making, our quality of presence and our ability to deal with stressful events.** This is a big deal. Amishi Jha describes our attention as the leader of the brain – where it goes, the rest of the brain's resources follow.

How do we gain control of our attention so that it's a good boss, serving us, rather than undermining or even derailing us? The good news is that there's hard evidence[3] that proves it is possible to train your attention. Even in high-octane military contexts, you can stay focused, be present, be more resilient and reduce trauma's effects.

+ReCharge!

The practice is attention training or mindfulness. It's dead easy to understand, but not so easy to sustain. Here's an activity to get you started:

Attention training – Application activity

1. Run an experiment where you do attention training for 10 minutes each day for a week. Why 10 minutes? Because "Our research shows that leaders who practiced the formal mindfulness exercises for more than 10 minutes per day fared much better on our key measures than those who didn't practice much or who relied on the informal practices alone."[42]

2. Decide when in the day you will do it and set up a reminder. If you're anything like us, you'll need it!

3. Choose a place where you won't be disturbed; some people do it on public transport with headphones on

4. Here's what you do: Close your eyes, relax, and sit upright. Place your full focus on your breath. Simply maintain an ongoing flow of attention on the experience of your breathing: inhale, exhale; inhale, exhale. To help your focus, stay on your breathing, count silently at each exhalation. Any time you find your mind distracted, simply release the distraction by returning your focus to your breath. Most important, allow yourself to enjoy these minutes

5. At the end of the week, answer these questions:
   (Note: please use scale of 1 for 'not at all' up to 5 for 'completely')

   a. To what extent do I feel calmer? (on a scale of 1-5)

   b. To what extent do I feel better able to control my attention? (1-5)

   c. Were there any downsides?

   d. Were there any other effects?

Attention training

> "Attention is very powerful in terms of affecting our perception. Even though it's so powerful, it's also fragile and vulnerable. And things like stress and mind-wandering diminish its power."

Amishi Jha

Two personal tips:

1. An additional benefit from a 'focus' perspective is that often when I do attention training, things that I have forgotten to do and didn't capture in my task management system will often pop into my mind. I keep a pen and paper by my side and quickly make a note of them, then return to focusing on my breathing, usually feeling relieved and a little bit calmer

2. If you've had an intense day and need to decompress in order to increase your chances of sleeping well, try doing your attention training either as part of the transition from work to life back at home, or as part of your pre-sleep routine.

"OUR ATTENTION IS LIKE A FLASHLIGHT YOU CAN DIRECT TO WHATEVER YOU CHOOSE."

REBEKAH BARNETT

Mind

How to focus
Managing distractions & flow
Attention training

Focus

Power of choice
Growth mindset
Managing attachments

Agility

Valuing self
Managing boundaries
Courageous conversations

Boundaries

AGILITY

POWER OF CHOICE

·

GROWTH MINDSET

·

MANAGING ATTACHMENTS

Power of choice

> "Everything can be taken from a man but one thing: the last of the human freedoms—to choose one's attitude in any given set of circumstances, to choose one's own way."
>
> **Viktor Frankl**

Choice is a very powerful concept. When applied more consciously, it can completely transform your life.

As you've seen from the previous chapter, the ability to choose how you spend your time and energy is a key determining factor of how you feel about your life, and most people – particularly busy people like yourself – struggle to consciously choose. Why? Mainly because the demands and obligations you face provide little time to reflect on how best to go about it.

A very important choice we can make is our attitude and response to a given set of circumstances. In particular, the ones that really challenge us and which we'd rather not be facing! It's in these situations that we learn most about ourselves and have the opportunity to grow and change.

There are three areas to consider when choosing our attitude:

THE PAST | THE PRESENT | THE FUTURE

How we frame our past presents the narrative of our life to ourselves and those around us. If we choose to hold on to the pain of what has happened before, then we will carry that with us. As Viktor Frankl, a survivor of Auschwitz and prominent psychologist, noted, **challenging events happen to everyone, but to continue the suffering long afterwards comes down to a choice.**

+ReCharge!

Likewise, if we're too fearful about the future, it will impact all our decisions accordingly. And if we are anxious about the present – often because we are fixated with what has occurred before or what might happen after – we stop enjoying the experience we have right in front of us.

It's a fine balancing act and needs conscious work to keep ourselves energized and positive, particularly when challenging events come, as they surely will. So it's vital that we choose our attitude, as it really affects our 'before, during and after' experience of living.

So how can we best do that?

There are two ways: letting go of the attachments you have, and developing a growth mindset. Along with the power of choice, and cultivating an openness to learning, these are the key elements in having an agile mind.

Perhaps the biggest issue holding us back is the nature of the things we're attached to. This does not mean just objects – often it's concepts, beliefs or judgements which hold a vice-like grip on our minds and prevent us from moving forward.

"May your choices reflect your hopes, not your fears."

Nelson Mandela

Power of choice

"You always have two choices: your commitment versus your fear."

Sammy Davis Jr.

Many traditions place an emphasis on letting attachments go on a daily basis, as they can be so pervasive; this practice helps us towards improved self-awareness. Its practitioners will say it helps them find calm in the present because they are able to clear the attachments they hold.

But first you need to be able to find out what those attachments are and the exercises in this chapter will help you do that.

Alongside consciously working on managing your attachments, it can be helpful to consciously cultivate a growth mindset. We look at how to do that in the next section.

A growth mindset looks at challenges as a source of learning, feedback as data to help us improve, and problems as opportunities. It is NOT cranky positivity which is overly optimistic and ungrounded. It involves consciously reshaping the way you think about challenges, helping you to learn and grow given the situation.

Again, it's a choice. And the more you practice it, the more you'll grow and the more energized you'll feel. The mindset of choosing a different response or way forward is a real boost to our self-esteem and energy levels. It also feels fantastic and is one of the most empowering habits you can develop.

WE ARE OUR CHOICES.

JEAN-PAUL SARTRE

Growth mindset

"Individuals who believe their talents can be developed (through hard work, good strategies, and input from others) have a growth mindset. They tend to achieve more than those with a more fixed mindset (those who believe their talents are innate gifts). This is because they worry less about looking smart and they put more energy into learning."

Carol Dweck
Harvard Business Review, 13 Jan 2016

Failure is an
opportunity to grow

GROWTH MINDSET

I can learn or do anything I want

Challenges help me to grow

Feedback is constructive

I'd like to try new things

Failure is the limit
of my abilities

FIXED MINDSET

I'm either good at it or I'm not

My potential is predetermined

When I'm frustrated I give up

I stick to what I know

+ReCharge!

Ever received some feedback (criticism) that hurt deeply?

Me too! It's horrible. This is why most of us will experience a slight increase in our heart rate when someone talks about the F-word.

Similarly, if you've ever tried to do something that felt important, and it didn't go as you hoped, for example a project or an important presentation or meeting, it can hurt. It normally hurts for one of two reasons:

1. The criticism or disappointment highlighted a blind spot, and it genuinely shocked you

2. The criticism or disappointment focused on an aspect of your skill, capabilities or character that is important to you. In other words, it undermined your sense of self – how you see and value yourself – and it may have evoked feelings of shame (yuk!)

Let's assume, a) you trust the accuracy of the feedback (most feedback is someone's opinion and may or may not be grounded in evidence), or b) your judgement about the results of the failed task or venture is grounded and balanced.

In that moment you have a choice. Do you acknowledge the feedback and disappointment (despite the pain) and explore the learning from the situation? Or, do you recoil, dismiss it, argue with it, pretend it didn't hurt and push the emotions down?

"Criticism may not be agreeable, but it is necessary. It fulfils the same function as pain in the human body. It calls attention to an unhealthy state of things."

Winston Churchill

Growth mindset

> "In a growth mindset, challenges are exciting rather than threatening. So rather than thinking, oh, I'm going to reveal my weaknesses, you say, wow, here's a chance to grow."
>
> **Carol Dweck**

One way of framing your response to this shocking feedback is the choice between embracing a fixed or growth mindset. It's not a one-off choice, but a series of choices we all consciously or unconsciously make. Whilst choosing a growth mindset may be good for us, that doesn't make it easy because:

"We all have our own fixed-mindset triggers. When we face challenges, receive criticism, or fare poorly compared with others, we can easily fall into insecurity or defensiveness, a response that inhibits growth. To remain in a growth zone, we must identify and work with these triggers."

Carol Dweck

The problem with repeatedly making fixed-mindset choices, from a resilience perspective, is that it leads to brittleness in our self-esteem. That in turn can lead us to play safe, which means playing small. This becomes unsatisfying and, over time, a massive energy-sapper. It is also very difficult to sustain, given the pace of change in most professionals' environments.

There are lots of benefits to be had in recognizing when your fixed-mindset 'persona' shows up, and what it says to make you feel threatened or defensive. Most importantly, over time you can learn to talk back to it, persuading it to collaborate with you as you pursue challenging goals.

+ReCharge!

Here is an activity to help you do this:

Growth mindset –
Application activity

1. Before proceeding, think about the contribution you most want to make in your life, maybe to your family, your community, or society. Why? Because "He who has a 'why' to live can bear almost any how" (Nietzsche). Carol Dweck found the same thing: when she asked people to call to mind the answer to the question above, afterwards they chose 30% more problems that challenged them, rather than playing small, safe and monochrome. Living with purpose is also part of our resilience model (see the EMOTION – MEANING section of this book), because we know that people who are clear about their purpose are more resilient than the drifters

2. Think of a recent time when you received some feedback (criticism) that hurt, or when you attempted something important that didn't go as you hoped

3. Draw 3 columns on a piece of paper[43]

4. Describe the facts in column 1. Imagine a video camera was recording the situation, e.g. "My boss sent me an email saying they were disappointed with the way the meeting went and could we fix a time to talk about it. I sent them a calendar invite for the next day. In the meeting, my boss started by asking me how I felt the meeting went and then told me clearly and precisely why they were so disappointed."

5. In column 2, describe:

   a. Your feelings/ reactions[44], e.g. "I felt humiliated or ashamed or embarrassed…"

   b. Your self-talk, e.g. "I am such an idiot to have thought I could pull this off", or "I always buckle under this kind of pressure"

   c. As you are describing the facts in column 1, you'll probably find the emotions of the situation returning. Not pleasant, but valuable for processing them and growing

Growth mindset

6. Column 3 is about sense-making. Answer the following questions:

   a. Have you had similar reactions to comparable past experiences? When? Is the trigger the same or similar?

   b. As you examine the self-talk that was going through your mind, how valid does it seem now?

      i. Do you need to test its validity? e.g. You may have felt that the feedback you received means you have blown your chances of getting promoted in the next round. Do you need to test that with someone?

      ii. Which of the self-talk do you need to re-write – something that supports a growth versus fixed mindset? Look at the examples to the side

Column 1 Facts	**Column 2** Reaction	**Column 3** Sense-Making

What can I say to myself?

INSTEAD OF...	TRY THINKING...
I'm not good at this	What am I missing?
I'm awesome at this	I'm on the right track
I give up	I'll use some of the strategies we've learned
This is too hard	This may take some time and effort
I can't make this any better	I can always improve so I'll keep trying
I just can't do Math	I'm going to train my brain in Math
I made a mistake	Mistakes help me to learn better
She's so smart. I will never be that smart	I'm going to figure out how she does it so I can try it
It's good enough	Is it really my best work?
Plan A didn't work	Good thing the alphabet has 25 more letters

Growth mindset

Three personal tips:

1. We like to do this in a space where you can express emotion without the need to self-censure

2. Don't rush this process. We find it helpful to have enough time to let your emotions and self-talk bubble up and breathe. If you are well connected to your emotions, allow a minimum of 30 minutes. If you struggle to express your emotions, allow longer

3. If you get stuck, seek help from someone you trust and who has proven themselves to be good at helping you think through difficult situations. If you don't have any friends like this, pay for someone to do it – a coach or a counsellor

You might be thinking, "Do I really want to dig up all those unpleasant emotions and relive an experience I hated the first time round?"

The answer is yes, because:

_____

"James Pennebaker has done 40 years of research into the links between writing and emotional processing. His experiments revealed that people who write about emotionally charged episodes experience a marked increase in their physical and mental well-being. Moreover, in a study of recently laid-off workers, he found that those who delved into their feelings of humiliation, anger, anxiety, and relationship difficulties were three times more likely to have been reemployed than those in control groups."

Susan David (2016), Harvard Business Review in 'A Vocabulary for Your Emotions.'

_____

REMAIN IN A GROWTH ZONE

CAROL DWECK

Managing attachments

> "Trees which don't bend with the wind eventually get uprooted by a big enough storm."

What is an attachment?

"It means clinging to people, beliefs, habits, possessions and circumstances. You feel emotionally attached to them and are unable and unwilling to let go, make changes, or get out of your comfort zone. It means lack of freedom, because you tie yourself to people, possession, habits and beliefs, and avoid change and anything new."

Remez Sasson[5]

The problem with attachments, from a resilience perspective, is that, like fixed mindsets, they lead to a rigidity in our responses to situations. It can reduce our flexibility. This is a problem, because adapting to circumstances is critical to being resilient. Trees which don't bend with the wind eventually get uprooted by a big enough storm.

+ReCharge!

Consider these common types of attachment:

Name of attachment	Description	Examples that spring to mind for you
To things happening a certain way	If you have a healthy imagination, it enables you to see how things could play out in a given situation. This helps bring direction (leadership) in situations. It's a huge asset; however, if you get too committed to your version of how things play out, you can become closed to alternative perspectives. This rigidity can cause you turmoil, especially if you are working with powerful people who don't accept your version of the future	
To being right	You may be over-attached to being right if you have a tendency to: • View your version of events as the most accurate, and err towards discounting other people's • Drive hard for people to acknowledge that you were right and they were wrong, especially in arguments	
To unthinking decisions and reactions	We all have 'emotional macros' or bits of 'emotional code' that run parts of the show. They can be helpful and assist us to make quick decisions and navigate situations with ease. Some can be unprocessed emotional pain or trauma being triggered. It can make us appear irrational, unthinking and reactive	

Managing attachments

Name of attachment	Description	Examples that spring to mind for you
To the way I've always done things	Many of us are creatures of habit and like things done in a particular way. When this becomes too important, and we react strongly to someone wanting to do things differently, it's a sign of rigidity or unhealthy attachment	
To making someone wrong	This is when we are very committed to keeping alive an explanation of someone's reasons, intentions or motives for doing something. This may be out loud in conversation or just in your own self-talk. It indicates you probably have unprocessed or unresolved hurt or are harbouring bitterness to the person (or group). It is making you rigid and causing you torment and that is sucking up energetic bandwidth that is better spent dealing with the present and future.	

+ReCharge!

Name of attachment	Description	Examples that spring to mind for you
To my stories (repeated patterns of self-talk)	If somebody mentions an individual or a situation, and a little audio file runs the same old message in your head, you may be living inside of a story. We all create them as a way of making sense of things that happen to us. It becomes a problem if those stories: • Become a truth that won't shift, even in the face of compelling contrary evidence • Are disempowering, for example, I'm sure you've met people who live inside of a \<victim\> story and it does nothing for their sense of power and resilience. You can change the word \<victim\> for any manner of words, such as \<I'm special\>, \<I deserve this\>, \<Everything will be fine\>, \<I'll never be loved\>, \<I'm not clever enough\>	

Managing attachments

> "Nothing ever goes away until it has taught us what we need to know."

Pema Chodron

All of these attachments drain energy and reduce flexibility.

Consider these generic signs of attachments:

1. If you say, "That's just who I am" as a way of explaining away behaviour

2. If you say, "That's just the way I do things" as a way of explaining away alternative approaches

3. If you repeatedly moan about someone or something

4. If you are disproportionately defensive of an attitude

"Often, the ideas that I am attached to do not make me feel better about myself or the world, but confirm limiting, negative beliefs that leave me feeling hurt, frustrated, angry, or overwhelmed. It's not my circumstances or reality that is frightening, overwhelming, or unfair— it's my thinking that makes them seem so."

Charlie Bloom 7 April 2014[6]

"Let go of your attachment to being right, and suddenly your mind is more open. You're able to benefit from the unique viewpoints of others, without being crippled by your own judgment."

Ralph Marston

Managing attachments – Application activity

Choose one of your attachments identified earlier – one that you'd love to break – and work through the three steps on the opposite page.

+ReCharge!

How to explore and break attachments:

STEP 01

Recognise and acknowledge that you might have an unhealthy attachment. It is very difficult to change something that is either out of awareness or which you don't accept is an issue. If in doubt, ask someone who knows you and who's opinion you trust: "Do I have a tendency to <Insert attachment>?"

STEP 02

Explore the attachment. At one point in time, the attachment will have made sense to you, at some level, even if it doesn't now. A great way of exploring this is to ask yourself the question, "Why does it make sense to <Insert attachment>?" Try to sense and feel into the answer, rather than to think and analyse.

Ask the question six or seven times – until there is no more energy in it.[7] You may find it easier to have someone ask you those questions. You may be surprised at what emerges. When I did this, when exploring why it made sense to play small, the response that eventually revealed itself was, "Because it is honouring to my dad". He had a deep-seated belief (based on some traumatising experiences) that the safest place to be was one where nobody noticed you.

It feels sad, but he genuinely believed that, and often said it aloud to us. By understanding where it came from, I was able to acknowledge that this 'attachment' worked for my dad, and to honour him, but it wasn't working for me. I chose to step out of it.

STEP 03

Craft some self-talk which supports you in embedding new beliefs around that issue. When the attachment kicks in next time, which it will, you can speak the new self-talk to it.

There may be habits or actions you need to develop to support you in breaking the attachment, but if you persist, it will lose its power. That was my experience with the attachment to playing small and not being noticed. You can read more about this in the MOOD – MANAGING SELF-TALK section of this book.

Mind

How to focus
Managing distractions & flow
Attention training

Focus

Power of choice
Growth mindset
Managing attachments

Agility

Valuing self
Managing boundaries
Courageous conversations

Boundaries

BOUNDARIES

VALUING SELF
·
MANAGING BOUNDARIES
·
COURAGEOUS CONVERSATIONS

Valuing self

> "No one can make you feel inferior without your consent."
>
> **Eleanor Roosevelt**

Perhaps the greatest gift anyone can give themselves, energy-wise, is self-love. In other words: actually treating yourself well, with positive care, thought and deed.

And yet most people struggle with this, because we can become our own worst critic. How does this happen?

We are invariably brought up with a series of cautious commands from our parents: be careful; watch out; take care; don't do this or that! They may have the best intentions in mind in order to help us avoid pain and discomfort, but if overdone, the pessimistic ratio of these instructions can tip over into our leading habitually cautious and fearful lives.

There has been considerable research in this area, and the concept that we possess a natural 'negativity bias' – or a tendency to focus more on negative events, judgements and beliefs than positive ones – only amplifies the issue. As Rick Hanson put it, "The mind is like Velcro for negative experiences and Teflon for positive ones", suggesting that this is a fundamental wiring of the brain almost irrespective of nurture or context.

All of this ends up draining a lot of valuable energy from us. But what can we do to help ourselves?

"Until you value yourself, you won't value your time. Until you value your time, you will not do anything with it."

M. Scott Peck

If we want more energy, we have to learn to push back and rebalance the ratio. In other words, we have to put more self-love into the equation and strengthen our sense of self.

+ReCharge!

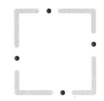

Those who have been lucky enough to receive more positive mental reinforcement from their environment (parents, teachers, family, friends, etc.) invariably have a healthier ratio of self-value; in other words they benefit from a stronger sense of self. In turn their choices and lives are often simpler, happier and more stable.

But they are the fortunate minority. **Most of us need to work on developing self-value and, in turn, reap the benefits in increased energy.** The good news is that with some practice you will reap the rewards pretty quickly.

To do this well there are a few practical areas to focus on and this chapter looks specifically at MANAGING BOUNDARIES and having COURAGEOUS CONVERSATIONS. You've seen in the first two chapters that if you don't value yourself enough, you can end up being a busy fool, allowing the obligations of others to dictate your agenda. This ends up having a detrimental, knock-on effect on our ability to get things done, or of people taking advantage of us.

The concept of managing our boundaries is simple: if you can start reminding people that you value your time, they will respect it more. And if you don't, they won't.

Another key element of valuing ourselves is our ability to engage with people on challenging issues. If we are unable do this constructively, we can become fragile and our resilience is affected. This is why it is important to be skillful at having courageous conversations.

> "Being deeply loved by someone gives you strength, while loving someone deeply gives you courage."
>
> **Lao Tzu**

"When I loved myself enough, I began leaving whatever wasn't healthy. This meant people, jobs, my own beliefs and habits – anything that kept me small. My judgement called it disloyal. Now I see it as self-loving."

Kim McMillen

Managing boundaries

> "If you don't learn to set boundaries in your life, other people will superimpose their priorities and values on you. The people who hate the fact that you're setting boundaries are the very ones who need them the most!"

Kris Vallotton

What are boundaries?

A boundary is simply a choice about how far either you will go, or you will let others go, in a domain of your life.

For example, you may set a boundary around the number of hours you are prepared to work in a day or week, the type of food you will or won't eat, or the way you treat your promises to people. Some boundaries might be fixed and never up for negotiation (for example, I never cancel a family holiday for work), whereas you might be prepared to flex others if the circumstances are exceptional (I don't check emails on a Sunday before 9pm, but I will if there is a critical work issue that requires my input).

Setting a boundary is simply a way of accepting that you have the power to make choices, and if you don't make healthy choices about what you will and won't do, other people will make those choices for you.

Why is it important to be clear about your boundaries?

It is a way of using the power you have. This is important for your sense of wellbeing, which feeds your resilience charge. If you are at people's beck and call, your resilience charge will be constantly depleted. Furthermore, we can sense whether someone is able to say no. If they don't, we normally respect them less than people who can say no (skilfully). It's a case of "They are a soft touch" versus "You can't take any liberties with them".

+ReCharge!

Boundaries have two primary purposes: to protect us from the outside world and to protect the outside world from us. In other words, they allow us to not be harmed by others, or to do harm to others.

Robert Frost famously said in a poem, "Good Fences Make Good Neighbours". He's making the point that boundaries between people in close proximity help them to get along better.

> "Good Fences Make Good Neighbours"
>
> **Robert Frost**

Setting and communicating boundaries

You can set some boundaries unilaterally: for example, what you will and won't watch on TV. With other boundaries, you may need to set them in collaboration with the people who will be impacted by them.

Say, for example, you have been pushing yourself too hard at work and you are getting ill far too frequently. You go and see the doctor, who does a number of tests and concludes that your immune system is depleted. They tell you that you need to replenish it by sleeping more and by working fewer hours; failure to address this is going to put you on a path to burnout. You need to discuss, propose and agree your boundaries with stakeholders at work and if you live with family members, them as well. The process of discussing and agreeing boundaries enrols important people into respecting them.

Managing boundaries

> "The truly free individual is free only to the extent of her own self–mastery... those who will not govern themselves are condemned to find Masters to govern them."

Stephen Pressfield

How healthy are your boundaries?

Dysfunctional boundaries usually manifest themselves in one of two ways:

1. We are too open/vulnerable (we allow others' words or actions to have too much influence upon us)

2. We are too impenetrable/invulnerable (we are too shut off and unable to truly connect with others and have great difficulty in accepting and processing others' emotions, thoughts, and behaviours)

You will find some additional questions on P.76 that will help you assess how healthy your boundaries between work and home are.

_____

> *"Do not justify, apologise for, or rationalise the healthy boundary you are setting. Do not argue. Just set the boundary calmly, firmly, clearly and respectfully."*

Crystal Andrus

_____

+ReCharge!

Managing boundaries – Application activity

1. Are there any areas in your life where setting clearer limits would help your levels of resilience charge?

2. In which areas of your life do people take liberties with you? What boundary could you set?

3. Is there an area of your life where you feel unhappy? Are there some clearer boundaries that you need to set?

Setting a boundary is a start, but if you can't enforce it, the boundary is meaningless.

You probably know from experience that there will always be people who want to test your boundaries! Being able to say no is a crucial skill in maintaining your resilience charge in these situations. Here are some more questions to consider:

4. How comfortable are you in skilfully saying no to attempts to infringe your boundaries? When did you last do it?

5. Are there any people that you struggle to say no to (and is it a reasonable versus unreasonable no)?

As sure as night follows day, a time is going to come when you need to talk to someone who is disrespecting your boundaries. That's when it is time to buckle up for a courageous conversation!

"The difference between successful people and really successful people is that really successful people say 'NO' to almost everything."

Warren Buffet

Courageous conversations

> "In conflict, time heals nothing; it causes hurts to fester."

Rick Warren

In addition to talking to someone who is disrespecting your boundaries, there are a whole host of other reasons why you may need to have a courageous conversation with someone. All are important to managing your resilience charge levels.

Here are a few:

- Someone has committed to do something for you, but the deadline has just whisked by and you've not heard a peep from them. It's a pattern, and it's making it difficult for you to deliver on your promises. It's causing you avoidable stress. You need to talk to them, to understand why it's happening, and to let them know that it's not acceptable to you.

- A senior person keeps disregarding what you say in meetings. You don't know why. You're finding it demeaning, and it's absorbing mental bandwidth that you can't afford to 'waste' like this.

- Someone in your team is under-performing and acting a little odd. Something's going on and you need to find out what. The team doesn't have enough capacity to carry an under-performer for much longer. You've been avoiding the conversation and it's been playing on your mind.

+ReCharge!

Most people avoid 'difficult' conversations like these for too long. The problem is that it absorbs mental bandwidth and this depletes our resilience charge. Here's an approach to having those 'difficult' conversations that has been tried and tested with some powerful and scarily aggressive people, and it works!

It works because it provides a structure for, on the one hand, being clear and assertive, but on the other, treating the other person with respect. Whilst we know from buttock-clenching experience that it works, you are still going to need to put your big boy or big girl pants on and step into the fire, hence why this section is called 'courageous' conversations.

"The courageous conversation is one you do not want to have."

David Whyte

Courageous conversations

The components of an effective courageous conversation

There is a model called OBRIFF which has been developed to describe the components of a highly effective approach to confronting an issue. It looks as follows:

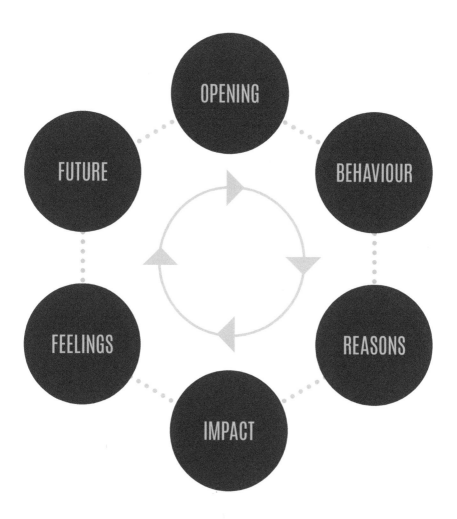

+ReCharge!

It is presented as a flow diagram because this makes it easier to isolate and explain each element. In reality, it is a lot more messy, and elements can flow back and forth or jump all over the place. Below is a description and illustration of each of the components:

OPENING

This is essentially about context setting. If you are meeting with the purpose of discussing a particular issue, then it is essential to set the tone for the conversation – one that will help rather than hinder the likelihood of a productive outcome.

Start by stating the purpose of the conversation, for example, "I'd like to talk about an issue that in my observation is making you less effective than you might be; I'll come on to the details in a minute."

Reiterate their value to you (if it is true and appropriate), for example, "I'm having this conversation because I rate you and I want you to be as effective as you can be."

State your intentions for the way you would like to conduct the conversation, for example, "I want to talk about this calmly and in a spirit of openness and I want to get your views on the matter."

All of this alerts the other person to the fact that a potentially difficult conversation is about to happen, but that it is going to be conducted openly, calmly and with dignity.

BEHAVIOUR

Start by describing as factually and as calmly as possible the behaviour you have seen; the facts.

For example, "Paul, I would like to have a chat about the accuracy of material that you are passing to me for review. In the last week, most of the documents needed significant re-work by me."

If the issue you want to talk about isn't as factual as this, then simply frame the issue as your 'perception' or 'gut feeling', for example, "Paul, I'm getting the impression that something is up. You don't seem your normal self?"

Courageous conversations

REASONS

Ask about their perspective, ask for a reaction or ask what their reasons were for doing the thing you are discussing; there may be some very good reasons that you are unaware of. Remember – everyone's behaviour makes sense to them, even if it seems odd to you.

For example, "I am wondering what your perspective is?" or "I'm wondering what is leading to this happening?"

The response you get to this question will determine where you go next in the conversation. You need to make a judgement based on the circumstances. This is where being agile and able to respond in the moment is a capability that can really help you.

IMPACT

Continue by exploring what the outcome or the impact of the behaviour was – the facts. Consider the impact on anyone involved in the issue including you and others. You could either:

Ask this as a question (if you want to use more of a coaching style and have the time and the right to do this), for example, "Paul, what do you think is the impact of your sending me documents that require significant re-work – on me and on my perception of you?"

Tell them (if you are short of time or don't think they have much of a chance of working it out, or it's not contextually appropriate), for example, "Paul, the impact of sending me documents that require significant re-work is that, a) it takes up much more of my time than I have planned for, so it causes me inconvenience, and b) it makes it harder for me to trust the quality of the work you produce, and that makes me want to avoid working with you."

+ReCharge!

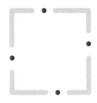

FEELINGS

Carry on by stating how you feel about the outcome (Disappointed? Shocked? Let down? Delighted? Proud?), for example, "That leaves me feeling frustrated."

This can feel vulnerable – because you are being open. It does, however, help to foster intimacy.

It can also be a potent lever for change, because when some people realise how what they are doing is affecting someone else, they may want to do something about it. If they have what can be termed psychopathic or narcissistic tendencies, it probably won't make the slightest bit of difference.

Furthermore, how you feel cannot be disputed by the other person.

"When I catch myself withholding the truth from a conversation, my instinct is to justify this behaviour by telling myself that I am really doing it for the other person's own good. Upon reflection, however, I find that my real motivation is an uncomfortable blend of both arrogance and fear. My arrogance is in play when I believe that the Talent is so fragile that he can't handle hearing something I believe to be true. But am I really so powerful? Is he really that breakable? My fear comes to the forefront when I convince myself that sharing the truth will produce some kind of emotional outburst from the Talent, making him unnecessarily uncomfortable. In reality I am protecting myself from the discomfort of intense emotional involvement."

Thompson G with Biro S (2006:69–81) 'Unleashed! Expecting greatness and other secrets of coaching for exceptional performance.' SelectBooks Inc., New York

---

Courageous conversations

FUTURE

Finish by agreeing what the individual will do about the issue in the future.

You can ask for ideas, or if the issue is about clarifying your standards for the way you expect to work, then tell them or explain, for example, "In future if you are not going to be able to hit a deadline that we agree – and let's face it, unexpected things often pop up – I ask that you let me know before, not after, the deadline, so we can think about alternatives."

Weblink, scan the code.

Visit here for a high-octane situation that one of us faced where OBRIFF was a game-changer:

CHAPTER SOURCES:

https://www.verywellmind.com/negative-bias-4589618 *(negativity bias)

https://en.wikipedia.org/wiki/Negativity_bias (negativity bias/effect)

+ReCharge!

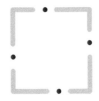

Courageous conversations – Application activity

Identify an important but difficult conversation that you've been avoiding:

1	Why is it important to have the conversation?
2	What's the worst thing that can happen?
3	Do you care enough about yourself, the issue or the person to do this?
4	What's the best outcome you can imagine?

Valuing ourselves is an area which impacts many aspects of our lives and we have only dealt with two aspects in this chapter. Another important area to work on is covered in MOOD – MANAGING SELF-TALK, which looks at dealing with the negative narratives we tell ourselves and dealing with our inner critic.

Body

Sleep management
Relaxation strategies
'Off' button

Restore

Energy diet
Exercise
Movement

Refuel

Finding joy
Develop learning openness
Sharing

Enjoy

RESTORE

SLEEP MANAGEMENT

·

RELAXATION STRATEGIES

·

'OFF' BUTTON

Sleep management

> Sleep is that golden chain that ties health and our bodies together.

Thomas Dekker

The single biggest factor in our wellbeing is sleep. It's so significant that if you are not looking after this, everything else you aim to improve in your life will lose impact. In fact, **a lack of sleep will kill you quicker than a lack of food** as the body starts adapting to fewer calories by shutting down parts of the system and conserving energy to survive. It has no such system when deprived of sleep. Without sleep, all hell breaks loose. Paranoia kicks in and the physiological system starts to unravel. In the hyper-busy world of most professionals – especially those with younger children – this is one area where major sacrifices are made and health and energy immediately suffer.

It has not helped that a lack of sleep was almost a badge of honour in most professions until recently. The importance of sleep has only now started to be realized. Elite athletes have understood the importance of a sleep strategy only too well and recognize its restorative effects. In fact, in their quest to maintain a competitive edge, sleep 'pods' at training facilities are now becoming a common site at major sporting clubs.

SLEEP IS AT THE HEART OF OUR **RESTORE** STRATEGY. IT WILL LOOK AFTER YOUR BODY AND BOOST YOUR ENERGY.

SLEEP IS THE BEST MEDITATION

DALAI LAMA

Sleep management

> "A good laugh and a long sleep are the two best cures for anything."

Irish Proverb

However, **the ability to switch off and relax outside of the time you are asleep is critically important** too. In this chapter, we offer a sleep strategy for you to try out, along with tools to help you switch off and relax. We believe that if you're able to experiment with all three of these aspects, you have an effective strategy to keep the body energized and healthy.

The key message here is that RESTORE begins with sleep and is supported by an ability to switch off and relax. To do this, you need to start valuing sleep and have a strategy for getting enough of it.

For some – again the lucky minority – a good's night sleep is easily accessible and to those people we would say how lucky you are! For the rest of us, like anything worthwhile, it needs some sound insights and a bit of work. Yet the results and benefits are immediate.

The following strategy has been researched and proven to work. I have added a few extra elements that I use to make it even more effective and you can see more detailed 'how' information in the resources cited at the end of this section.

I can testify that over the past few years it has transformed my wellbeing. Note – you don't need to do all the elements every night, but they do work very well together as a sleep routine. Our advice is to give this a go for the next four weeks. After that you can then reflect on your experience before deciding how you take it forward and make it your own.

+ReCharge!

Sleep Strategy:

1 Have a daily cut-off time for caffeine intake (allow 8hrs before your bedtime)

2 Have a firm cut-off time for digital appliances (at least one hour before bedtime)

3 Have a book to read after digital cut-off time if necessary

4 Eat food that encourages good sleep and digestion before bedtime (E.g. kiwifruit, tart cherries and malted milk drinks[8])

5 Practice sleep yoga exercises before getting into bed

6 Use a coherent breathing technique (see the 'Relaxation Strategies' exercise) to relax yourself to sleep

7 Sleep in a room slightly cooler (-1.5°C) than room temperature

8 Invest in a mattress and pillow which exceed your comfort expectations

Sleep management

FACT:
A study by
Sainsbury's
found that
the quality
of sleep had
by far the
strongest
association
with
wellbeing of
any lifestyle
factor that
we can
control.

Additional elements:

1. Consider a safe, herbal sleep supplement, such as Valerian, to aid sleep

2. Consider Melatonin supplements from your pharmacy to help induce sleep hormones

3. If your mind is still racing, consider the following mental exercise to switch off:

   a. Choose a word with between 4-6 letters. Any word will do, e.g. HOUSE

   b. Starting with the first letter (H), list all the words you know that start with this letter

   c. Once you've run out of words for each letter, move onto the next one (O)

   d. Repeat until complete

4. Finally, if your mind is still racing - do NOT stay in bed but get up and write down all of the things that are ON your mind. By jotting them down you will be both consciously and sub-consciously putting them to bed too!

"TENSION IS WHO YOU THINK YOU SHOULD BE. RELAXATION IS WHO YOU ARE."

CHINESE PROVERB

BODY – RESTORE

Relaxation strategies

"Learn how to exhale, the inhale will take care of itself."

Carla Melucci Ardito

The problem

You've been working intensively and feel wired. You know you need to bring the RPM's (Revs Per Minute) down, but when you stop work, your mind is still firing thoughts and impulses like bullets out of a gun. There's a tension and alertness (a feeling of being pumped) in your body. It all makes it very hard to relax and switch off.

The solution

Breathing!

It sounds (too) simple.

And yes, it is simple to do, but counter-intuitive in the 'wired' moment.

The technique we are about to share is used by many professionals who need to calm themselves down physiologically, often in high-pressure situations, in order to make quality decisions and perform at their best.

It was part of the solution that helped the England national football team overcome its quarter-century jinx of losing penalty shootouts in major tournaments[9]. It's also used by many special forces operatives who have to handle life-threatening situations such as getting lost in enemy territory.

The technique is called 'Coherent breathing'.[10]

It brings you out of a 'fight or flight' response into a state of 'relaxed alertness' where you are present in the moment but with a much wider perspective of the situation you are in. By contrast, when we are in a more stressed state of mind, we tend to focus far more narrowly, experiencing 'tunnel vision', losing our perspective.

+ReCharge!

Regaining control of our breathing is the one thing we do have control over, even in the most challenging of circumstances. This then gives us a sense of agency that is often missing from the uncertainty of situations we find ourselves in.

What is Coherent breathing?[11]

A regular in-breath (normally around a count of five) and the same out-breath restores a state of 'relaxed alertness'. If we just want to be 'relaxed', then a longer out-breath leads us to a state of 'rest and repose'.

You'll need to do it for about ten minutes.[12]

Experiment with it

Try it the next time you feel 'wired', overwhelmed or pumped, when you either need to compose yourself to make a sensible appraisal of the situation and decide on the best way forward, or you simply need to relax as part of transitioning into an out of work mode.

Breathing is at the core of relaxation. However, there are many other strategies to help you relax too. In the BODY – ENJOY section of this book, you will explore activities and areas in your life which will also contribute to helping you and your system relax. The important thing to bear in mind is that we need to have a variety of strategies available to us to reduce our RPM.

> "Sometimes the most productive thing you can do is relax."
>
> **Mark Black**

'Off' button

> "Your mind will answer most questions if you learn to relax and wait for the answer."
>
> **William Burroughs**

Most people know that it makes sense to find your 'Off' button when you get home from work, but sometimes that's easier said than done, especially when you are feeling wired after an intense day!

Finding 'Off' is an essential element of BODY, and failing to attend to it can make it difficult to sleep deeply. It can also rob you of that feeling of being properly rejuvenated. Furthermore, people around you at home sense you aren't fully present for them, which isn't great for relationships.

If you don't pay attention to this, it can gradually start to adversely affect your energy levels. If it continues, you can get pushed into a dangerous burnout zone.[13]

> *"A frog tossed into a pot of boiling water will jump out, but a frog in a pot of water that is slowly heated will cook. It grows more and more accustomed to untenable circumstances. Like the frog, people who try to satisfy ever-increasing demands by drawing on ever-decreasing energy sources will become numb to the consequences of the choices you are making."*
>
> **Tony Schwartz[14]**

+ReCharge!

How can you find 'Off'? You can use a combination of new habits and lessons from cognitive behavioural therapy:[15]

1. **Focus on what you'll do instead.** Many people fail to change their behaviour because they focus on what they don't want to do, rather than on what they will do instead. You cannot create a habit to avoid an action. Furthermore, when you set negative goals, you must constantly be vigilant about your behaviour, or you will end up doing the thing you are trying to avoid. Instead, you need to focus on what you are going to do. In the case of switching off from work, be specific, e.g. "On Tuesday evening at 7.45pm, I am going to take Jake to his Karate class, and I will sit and read a novel during the class".

2. Sometimes though, your downtime may be **invaded by intrusive thoughts about work.** In this case, you want to be prepared so that you don't keep ruminating about upcoming work. One way to deal with intrusive thoughts is to have an 'IF-THEN plan at the ready: 'IF I start thinking about work when I'm relaxing, THEN I will acknowledge it, have a little chuckle, capture anything that requires action and re-engage with what I was doing.'

3. **Change your environment to support your new behaviour and discourage the old one.** A drinker doesn't try to quit alcohol while leaving booze in their fridge. Similarly, someone trying to set healthier work-life boundaries doesn't leave themselves easy prey to work interruptions. Yes, I am suggesting you actually turn your devices off; make it hard to do that work. When I have to switch my phone back on to check it, it interrupts the addictive urge and makes me think about whether I really want to do it. Use the environment to help you by having a space at home that you will never use to work. The more that you associate this spot with things that do not involve work, the easier it will be to use this area to get away from work thoughts. Ask other people to help you stay away from work. Give them permission to challenge you (and don't get annoyed with them when they do). Find activities that distract you from work-related thoughts.

'Off' button

4. **Consider if your boundaries are too leaky (or non-existent).** In the section on BOUNDARIES we introduced the notion of setting parameters that limit what you will and won't do. This thinking is extremely useful when it comes to putting in place boundaries that will help you to relax, for example:

   a. What's your default cut-off time for *checking* work emails and messages?

   b. What's your default cut-off time for *responding* to work emails and messages?

   c. What's the maximum number of work-related social events you'll attend per week (or per month if that's a rhythm that's more pragmatic for you)?

   d. What's the maximum number of nights you'll be away from home with work per week (or per month if that's a rhythm that's more pragmatic for you)?

   e. How late are you prepared to work, especially if the cause is someone else's poor planning or failure to think ahead?

   f. What's the maximum number of hours you'll work per week (or per month if that's a rhythm that's more pragmatic for you)?

For many people, the answer to these questions is "I don't know". In effect they are giving others the power to set the limits on these critical issues which influence our ability to find 'Off'.

+ReCharge!

Here are some ideas to help you apply these principles:

'Off' button – Application activity

- Capture in writing any of the ideas above that you want to experiment with. Say when you will start. Consider letting any significant others know. Ask them to help you

- Deepen your understanding of why you struggle to switch off by creating two columns in your journal:

  1. What do I get from never properly switching off from work?

  2. What does it cost me?

  - Critically analyse how true each point is in column 1

  - Ask if you can afford to continue accepting each cost in column 2

SLEEP STRATEGY RESOURCES:

www.fitnessmagazine.com/health/sleep/what-to-eat-for-better-sleep/
(Foods to aid sleep – scroll down in article to find them)

www.mindbodygreen.com/0-28550/have-insomnia-these-yin-yoga-poses-will-put-you-right-to-sleep.html (Sleep yoga)

www.youtube.com/watch?v=TcF2TSuQEn4 (Sleep yoga video)

www.youtube.com/watch?v=YRPh_GaiL8s (4-7-8 Breathing)

www.carpediembeds.com/no/ (Life-changing comfortable beds)

www.ncbi.nlm.nih.gov/pmc/articles/PMC4394901/ (Research on Valerian)

www.amazon.com/Best-Sellers-Health-Personal-Care-Valerian-Herbal-Supplements/zgbs/hpc/3767221 (Recommended Valerian products)

Body

Sleep management
Relaxation strategies
'Off' button

Restore

Energy diet
Exercise
Movement

Refuel

Finding joy
Develop learning openness
Sharing

Enjoy

REFUEL

ENERGY DIET
·
EXERCISE
·
MOVEMENT

Energy diet

> "I finally realized that being grateful to my body was key to giving more love to myself."
>
> **Oprah Winfrey**

Our bodies are naturally very resilient. Generally, they can heal and recover from most things and return to their natural state of equilibrium (energy and health) if we give them a regular chance to do so.

To do this requires balance, moderation and sometimes reducing obstacles that get in the way of this recovery process. Our approach is to sustain your body as long as possible with energy and agility. Our bodies were not designed to last forever, yet with some care – and a little luck – they can happily transport us without too many major issues until it's time to leave them behind.

While there are no guarantees of a smooth journey, we strongly believe that it is much more likely if you begin to consider a few factors.

Firstly, the body is constantly giving us messages about our levels of well-being. If we start to notice these – and begin to attend to these signals – we will create a much more harmonious experience. This means recognizing fatigue and giving yourself time to recover. It means being familiar with hunger and snacking properly. It also means knowing what lethargy feels like and moving properly to re-energize. Put simply, it requires a level of consciousness that can be challenging when we get too busy, especially with a young family.

+ReCharge!

To help with this, start practicing and checking in with some simple questions to yourself on these areas.

Energy diet – Application activity

- How hydrated do I feel?
- How are my energy levels?
- How tired do I feel and where do I feel it?
- Where am I feeling tension?
- How hungry am I feeling and how do I know?

The next thing to consider is how unique your body is. Each body metabolizes differently, which is why there is no single diet that works for everyone. The key here is to **start understanding how your body responds to certain foods by creating mini-experiments**. Find out what your body likes and doesn't like, and enjoy the process while doing so.

The final thing to consider is **what you can start reducing or cutting out**. Bad habits run deep, and the consequences can be extremely dangerous to our energy and wellbeing. We now know conclusively that certain things will have a negative compounding impact on our health: processed foods, too much meat and alcohol certainly fall into this category. So beginning to moderate these will go a long way towards improving your wellbeing.

"You need to listen to your body because your body is listening to you."

Phil McGraw

"Your body is your best guide. It constantly tells you, in the form of pain or sensations, what's working for you and what's not."

Hina Hashmi[16]

Energy diet

> "Let food be thy medicine, thy medicine shall be thy food."

Hippocrates

A diet strategy to boost energy & health

If you're serious about making changes to your diet, we would recommend keeping a 7-day food diary first to set it up for success.

Unless you've kept a food diary before, it is very easy to forget exactly what you put in your mouth throughout the day. It is also a very effective way of raising your awareness of automatic snacking habits that might be blind spots and preparing you to make the necessary changes you want to action.

We've found it works best (and most accurately) when you update it during the day after meals or snacks, rather than attempting to remember it all at the end of the day. Once you've seen the reality of your activity over a 7-day period, we would then suggest designing mini 7-day experiments to try out what foods you want to avoid and what foods you would like to add.

"The truth will set you free, but first it may make you miserable!"

Rick Warren

+ReCharge!

For the first 7 days, keep it simple and only choose a few things in both add/avoid areas. You can increase the choices each 7 days and build these up over a longer period.

At the end of a month (28 days), you should be able to notice how your body is responding and can then more easily decide on the changes you want to consider making going forward. So take the pressure off and wait until the end before committing to any long-term decisions.

Foods to add:

The following are proven to significantly boost your energy while still being good for you. Additionally, most of these foods are easy to digest and lead to increased sleep quality too:

- Almonds
- Apples
- Bananas
- Beans
- Brown rice
- Chia seeds
- **Eggs** 97% protein
- Green tea
- Honey
- Limes
- Natural yoghurt

- Oatmeal
- Oranges
- Quinoa
- Salmon
- Spinach
- Sweet potatoes
- Water
- **Probiotic foods** for gut health
- **Organic foods** where possible

"My weaknesses have always been food and men — in that order."

Dolly Parton

Energy diet

> "If it came from a plant, eat it; if it was made in a plant, don't."

Michael Pollan

Foods to avoid:

What you avoid is just as important as what you put in, and this is where a food diary is vital to notice all elements of your diet. It sounds boring but the key to maintaining your energy through food is balance. The occasional blow-out or relapse on the 'avoid' list is to be expected; just don't make it a habit if you want to maintain your energy levels.

Here are the following to consider avoiding:

- Alcohol
- (White) bread
- Coffee
- Dairy (milk and cheese)
- Energy drinks
- Milk chocolate
- Red meat and processed foods
- Rice and pasta (refined)
- Sweets/candy

Our 30-day journey:

Under the supervision of an expert diet coach (Michele Kaye, author of *Eat, Dance & Shine*), I recently conducted a 30-day lowish-fat, vegetable-based diet designed to boost energy.

The results were astounding. I lost 3 kilos, my 'gut' actually disappeared, my eczema cleared up, I slept better, stressed less and generally bounced around a bit more.

> "We never know what is enough until we know what is more than enough."
>
> **Billie Holliday**

Now, was all this down to the diet? Maybe not, but the coincidence was eerie. The biggest difference was not falling asleep every evening immediately after supper and instead spending that time with my young daughter, as well as being able noticeably to focus more on tasks during the day.

+ReCharge!

The results were so good that I've decided to keep this up going forward.

30-day journey preparation:

1. Start with a 7-day food diary to audit your intake before you begin

2. This gives you a week to plan and think through some recipes or combinations that appeal. Plus, it highlights some of the snacks and foods you want to avoid

3. Make sure you go and buy ingredients in advance to get you through the first few days of the opening experiments and bin any temptations ('avoid' list stuff) that may lie around. It's fine to have a few lurking; just accept that if they are available, they are likely to be eaten/drunk

4. Find a buddy to join you on the journey. It makes it more fun

5. Give yourself a cut-off period. You can extend this if you want to continue making the changes

6. Realise that 'making it tasty' is the key to maintaining anything without it feeling like torture. And the good news is there are a load of resources that help with this (See 'Resources' at the end of this section)

> "A good rule to remember is, 'Could our ancestors eat it?' or 'Was it available thousands of years ago?' If not, it is probably not that good for us."
>
> **MK Lifefit**

> *"If you keep good food in your fridge, you will eat good food."*
>
> **Errick McAdams**

BODY – REFUEL

Energy diet

Here is a recommended menu for boosting energy, performance & health:

BREAKFAST OPTIONS

Bananas · Blueberries and acai

Dandelion/Green tea · Fresh smoothie

Honey · Oatmeal with raisins

Omelette with red peppers · Yoghurt

LUNCH OPTIONS

Fresh fruit, nuts (almonds)

Mixed leaf salad with any of: avocado, chicken, tuna, feta, peppers, chillies

Salmon with quinoa or beans

Sushi (mix with sashimi and edamame to reduce amount of rice)

DINNER OPTIONS

Chorizo sausages (90% meat)
with sweet potato and kale (or other greens)

Curries (with brown basmati rice) **and spinach**

Wholewheat pasta with most pasta sauces
(don't worry about carb content – the percentage of sugars is the thing to watch for)
and a mixed salad

+ReCharge!

COOKING OILS & TIPS

Cook with coconut oil and use olive oil to dress sauces instead

Bake instead of fry and **steam** instead of boil

. . . .

SAUCES

Use **tamarind**, **lime pickles**, **lime juice** & fresh home-made **mayonnaise**

. . . .

SNACKS

Dark chocolate (70%+)

Healthy 'crisps' – chickpea, lentil, etc

Hummus – loads of different types now and all yummy

Oatmeal biscuits

RESOURCES:

https://www.youtube.com/watch?v=YMOxX-U9hvg **(healthy omelette)**

https://www.youtube.com/watch?v=A6mxdKtJOyI **(healthy salad dressings)**

'Eat, Dance, Shine – how to come alive, gain energy and push back the years' **by Michele Kay available via Amazon**

Exercise

> "It is exercise
> alone that
> supports
> the spirits
> and keeps
> the mind in
> vigor."
>
> **Marcus Tullius Cicero**

Ever had the experience of being wiped out after a demanding day? You're tempted to grab some takeaway food and your alcoholic beverage of choice, and crash in front of the TV.

Somehow you resist and do some exercise instead. Afterwards you feel transformed. You sleep deeply too. That's because:

"A single workout will immediately increase levels of neurotransmitters like dopamine, serotonin and noradrenaline. That is going to increase your mood right after that workout. My lab showed that a single workout can improve your ability to shift and focus attention, and that focus improvement will last for at least two hours."

Neuroscientist Wendy Suzuki[17]

Additionally, a critical dimension to managing your resilience is increasing your chances of remaining healthy and staying alive! Having an exercise regime is fundamental to that.

"Middle-aged and older people who live sedentary lives are up to two and a half times more likely to die early. The risk remained even if sitting was broken up by standing and walking, typical of a desk-based job. Light activity such as cooking or washing-up could help lessen the risk. People who did regular physical activity of any intensity were about five times less likely to die early than those who were not physically active."

Rosie Taylor[18]

The most important thing is to find something you enjoy doing. This way you'll probably keep it up when the dark

+ReCharge!

nights set in. So think deeply about what that might be and commit to giving it a go.

Remember that from the age of 45 onwards, the body needs to maintain muscle, otherwise it starts to waste away and is increasingly hard to get back. So also consider some workouts to maintain muscle. You don't have to go to a gym, and it can be done at home.

"What if I told you there was something that you can do right now that would have an immediate, positive benefit for your brain including your mood and your focus? And what if I told you that same thing could actually last a long time and protect your brain from different conditions like depression, Alzheimer's disease or dementia. Would you do it? Yes! I am talking about the powerful effects of physical activity."

Neuroscientist Wendy Suzuki[19]

The rule of thumb is you want to exercise three to four times a week for a minimum of 30 minutes a session, and you want to make some of it aerobic exercise.

A word of warning

Be aware of significantly increasing the stress loads on your body. If you have any doubt about how much is healthy for your body, consult a qualified medical practitioner.

> "Reading is to the mind what exercise is to the body."
>
> **Joseph Addison**

Movement

> "Sitting still for nine and a half hours a day raises the risk of early death."
>
> **Rosie Taylor[20]**

The problem

The body needs to move. And today's society and working environment make that harder than ever. It's slowly killing us. As one health professional told me when we were researching this, 'A lack of movement is the new smoking'.

If you're like most professionals, you'll be sitting around a lot.

We asked one group we worked with to track how much time they spent seated. It averaged out at 12 hours plus a day (work and home total).

If this is you, then **the most important thing is to start moving regularly.** Make sure you have a 60-minute alert which reminds you to get up, stretch, and grab a glass of water. Just by doing this simple practice of moving and hydrating will help prevent premature aging and boost your mood significantly.

Next start considering how to increase your movement when you have to go places. And start challenging some habits:

1. Where can you walk (run, cycle, even swim) instead of taking transport? Even if it is part of the journey?

2. Can you use the staircase instead of the lift?

3. How about considering a stand-up desk?

+ReCharge!

To help boost your motivation, consider buying an activity monitor, as they help you to see progress with steps and heartrate. And set it to 10,000 steps, which is the recommended daily amount you need to stay healthy.

There are other problems with being seated and working on a computer for lengthy periods, which can cause neck and back pain. To alleviate this, do the following:

- Stretching practice

- Pilates or yoga

- Every 20 minutes, look 20 feet away. It helps your eye muscles and reduces headaches

> "If we could give every individual the right amount of nourishment and exercise, not too little and not too much, we would have found the safest way to health."
>
> **Hippocrates**

Body

Sleep management
Relaxation strategies
'Off' button

Restore

Energy diet
Exercise
Movement

Refuel

Finding joy
Develop learning openness
Sharing

Enjoy

ENJOY

FINDING JOY

·

DEVELOP LEARNING OPENNESS

·

SHARING

BODY – ENJOY

Finding joy

> "People rarely succeed unless they have fun in what they are doing."
>
> **Dale Carnegie**

A powerful source of energy is having things to look forward to which give us joy.

Sadly, one of the costs of being too 'busy' is that we can overlook these often 'small' things and our lives begin to feel considerably less enjoyable. If we take it too far, we can end up losing our mojo completely.

Anhedonia is a medical condition on the rise. It has helped in the diagnosis of depression and is categorized by an 'inability to feel pleasure in normally pleasurable activities.' In other words, it is the complete absence of joy, and any person who has experienced intense periods of busyness or stress can relate to it.[21]

Research into this condition has revealed that there are two important aspects to consider: difficulty in 'wanting' or looking forward to something, and then difficulty in 'liking' or enjoying the experience.

The cure is simple: if we are able to diarise stuff we really enjoy doing, and then make sure we do enough of it, we will experience a lot of positive energy. This might sound deceptively simple, but most people with busy lives and family obligations regularly fail to enjoy doing things. If this resonates, then this chapter is for you.

In this chapter we will introduce you to the habit of FINDING JOY regularly on your own and as a shared activity (SHARING). We will also deepen the practice of enjoyment to include how you learn.

Learning new things is a practice with limitless joy, yet this can also suffer during particularly busy periods of our lives. This chapter will introduce you to the concept of how to DEVELOP LEARNING OPENNESS, which will boost your ability to recharge by learning smart in different ways that are easily available to us.

+ReCharge!

Finding joy –
Application activity

This is one of the simplest applications of the RECHARGE! model but can make an immediate impact. Put simply, we get energy from doing the things we love to do. And the more we do, the happier and more energized we become, which ends up making life that much more fun and enjoyable.

Reflect on the top 5 things you absolutely, without a shadow of doubt, love doing more than anything else (and leave your work off the list for now...)

Tim's list:

1. Dancing with my daughter
2. Cooking for friends
3. Playing squash
4. Surfing
5. Writing

Your list:

1.
2.
3.
4.
5.

Now spend a few moments and imagine yourself doing these things and feel the smile come across your face.

So, now it's time to start having some fun and giving yourself a real energy boost by getting on with creating your list. ENJOY!

Here's all you need to do. Get out your diary and think about where you can schedule some of this stuff. Right now.

BODY – ENJOY

Develop learning openness

> "Learning is a treasure that will follow its owner everywhere."

Chinese Proverb

Get more energy from how you learn

The endorphic rush or 'buzz' we get from stretching ourselves and mastering new things is well-known and has been extensively researched. The challenge facing us when we get too busy is that we stop learning and go on autopilot in order to survive. This quickly leads to inertia, despondency and a lack of drive and energy. Sound familiar?

Learning openness is the idea that if we are open to learning in different ways, then we can seriously boost our energy reserves, as well as our motivation and enjoyment. Its purpose is to foster our ability to be curious, self-aware and reflective. And according to Flaum & Winkler ('Improve your ability to learn' Harvard Business Review, June 2015) this is best done by cultivating our learning agility, as well as coaching it in others.

So how do you do this? **Here are 7 behaviours associated with it to help you:**

Curiosity. Being curious about the world is very energizing. Anyone with small children can relate to this, as it can also be exhausting for parents! Seriously though, if we are able to get beneath the surface and understand issues, themes, motivations and challenges around us, it can lead to great insights. It is also a lot of fun. So, how can you benefit from being more curious around you, particularly in the areas that challenge you? For example, by simply asking 'what is this challenge teaching me?' can energize you.

Innovating. Finding new ways of doing things makes us feel good and gives us energy. Ask yourself, 'How else could I do this?' before you execute something. It doesn't mean you need to do all of these things – it merely invites you to explore them before finding another potential solution.

+ReCharge!

Understanding. Seek to identify patterns in complex situations. Find the similarities between current and past projects. Cultivate calm through meditation and other techniques. Enhance your listening skills – learn to understand rather than respond. Ask yourself, what are the themes here?

Reflecting. Learn to ask yourself, 'How did I handle that situation that was particularly effective?' And 'What are the three or four things I could have done better here?' Make sure the question is answered openly and not simply 'Could I have done better?' This also encourages other people to speak up. This reflective practice is often called journaling. Many people use either a paper or digital notebook to capture these thoughts. Elsewhere, we reference other ways to use your journal.

Risking. We all need some time out of our comfort zone to freshen things up. Look for stretch assignments where success is not guaranteed. Have another look around you and see what you could put yourself forward for. Start creating learning 'goals' to achieve.

Self-awareness. How well do you know yourself. How well do you know your strengths? How about your blind spots? Developing an awareness in both these areas and working on them gives us a lot of confidence and energy. Consider getting a personality profile[22] to help guide you here.

Avoid Defending. Acknowledge your failures (maybe from the stretch assignments) and capture those lessons. Most people admire those who are able to dust themselves down and move on. Be one of those types and let go of any 'baggage' you might be carrying through being defensive. It's very draining to be defensive – learn to let go of it.

"The more that you read, the more things you will know. The more that you learn, the more places you'll go."

Dr. Seuss

Develop learning openness – Application activity

Practice one of these behaviours every week, for the next 7 weeks.

Sharing

> '**Happiness is only real when shared.**'
>
> **Chris McCandless,**
> last diary entry – from the film, *Into the Wild*

There are **four dimensions to sharing which can boost your resilience 'charge':**

1. Sharing your learning

2. Sharing things you enjoy doing (unless doing it alone is what makes it so enjoyable)

3. Sharing more of yourself (your inner world)

4. Sharing your resources and assets

We are going to look briefly at each one and offer some ideas to experiment with them. These have the aim of seeing if you can squeeze more juice from these sources of vital resilience energy.

Sharing your learning

We've just been talking about learning openness, and how learning something new can be deeply energizing.

Have you had the experience of sharing what you've been learning, and then you either see other people benefiting from it, or you see that they find it interesting and engaging and as a result you have a nourishing conversation?

It has an energetic kick-back for you.

On the following page are four ideas to experiment with which can activate this source of energy:

+ReCharge!

Sharing – Application activity

1. Experiment with:

  a. Asking your friends what they have been learning. If they are dead-heads and say "nothing", push them for what they have been learning from the experiences of living – this week/month/or through a big event (e.g. a company restructure)

  b. Sharing what you have been learning and gauging how interested people are and whether they are open to further conversations

2. Where you had a significant shared experience with someone, such as being part of a shockingly bad meeting, initiate a conversation afterwards where you analyse and debrief what happened, whether you could have handled it differently or intervened more effectively. Just watch out it doesn't turn into a BMW session (Blaming, Moaning and Whining)!

3. If you are a leader, at one of your team meetings, either arrange in advance for someone to do a short teach-back on a recent learning experience, or lead one yourself, e.g. attending a conference or workshop, doing some formal study, reading a book, working on a project, etc. Keep the presentation part short, and have some questions prepared to lead a discussion afterwards. Notice the energetic impact on yourself and ask others how it was for them

4. If you are a leader, have a resilience 'moment' at the next team meeting. What's one of those? It is taken from the world of safety management and is a brief talk about a specific subject at the beginning of a meeting. They have the effect of saying, 'this is important'. They can be done in a variety of ways but are typically a brief (2-5 minute) discussion on a resilience-related topic. Ideally, they should:

  a. Be personal, showing your personal connection to the topic and ideally giving some self-disclosure

  b. Share some successes – either yours or others'

  c. Include a question which invites people to share their thoughts or experiences about the topic

With the latter two, you will need to provide a context for your team that helps them to understand why you are focusing on it.

Sharing

> "Pull up a chair. Take a taste. Come join us. Life is so endlessly delicious."

Ruth Reichl

Sharing things you enjoy doing (unless doing it alone is what makes it so enjoyable)

Earlier in this chapter, we talked about the importance of doing things you love – things that you look forward to and which bring you joy and life.

Sometimes, doing that activity with others who share the love of it can multiply the joy and energy it brings. Our suggestion is to experiment with this.

For example, I love cycling. I've got four bikes! I've done several solo cycling holidays. I mostly love cycling alone in the beautiful countryside where I live, and I can feel it nourishing my soul as well as pushing my body. One of my adult sons, who normally lives away from home, stayed at my house during the Covid-19 lockdown. We got into the habit of doing a 2 to 4-hour cycle ride together most Sundays. What fun! It multiplied the normal joy of cycling (and pushed me to breaking point!).

Here's some ideas for you to consider:

- What do you love doing to relax?
- Who could you experiment doing it with to see if it enhances the joy? (It may not. No problem – it's an experiment)

Sharing more of yourself (your inner world)

A genuine and authentic connection with others soothes our souls. It can be beautiful.

If you cast your mind back to the last real conversation you had with someone, you'll probably start to feel the soothing, energizing glow that you experienced at the time.

+ReCharge!

This is why we are devoting a later section of this book to building meaningful connection with others (CONNECT – MEANINGFUL RELATIONSHIPS).

It is much harder to build and sustain a healthy level of resilience charge alone. For example, medical research[23] has shown us that loners are:

- more susceptible to physical illness

- more vulnerable to mental ill-health, and

- die younger than people with rich relationships

Here's one practice to experiment with: **Being responsibly vulnerable.**

What does that mean?

When you are chatting with people, if it feels appropriate, share what's going on in your internal world. Experiment with being gradually, but increasingly, more real and open with people and see what the impact is:

- You could share something you're finding difficult

- You could talk about something you've particularly enjoyed

- You could disclose something you're particularly proud about

Here's a small personal example. The other weekend, I was mentally bogged down with a piece of client work and was struggling to find a way through it. I told my spouse about it (who isn't a businessperson). I was surprised how my perspective shifted and how much better I felt!

> "In Social Chemistry, Yale professor Marissa King explains that your social connections are a strong predictor of your cognitive functioning, resilience, and engagement."
>
> **True Friends at Work**
> - Alison Beard HBR
> July–August 2020

BODY – ENJOY

Sharing

> "It ain't no fun if the homies can't have none."

Snoop Dogg

Sharing your resources and assets

A lot of research shows that we get more satisfaction from giving as opposed to receiving.

Really?

Yes!

Both experience and research proves it.

Starting with your experience, think back to a time when you voluntarily helped someone out with your time or resources. You probably felt good about yourself and felt pleased you'd done it, even though it may have been costly.

Research[24] shows that acts of generosity and kindness release dopamine, and we know from the earlier REFUEL sections on EXERCISE and MOVEMENT how this makes us feel energized.

For example, I've got a mate who's been out of work for a while. His back-up resources are getting depleted; he's struggling mentally and emotionally. He and his wife share a computer, and since she's using it to earn money, she has first claim on it. That's not helping him when he's writing job applications and trying to do research.

I had a spare hi-spec laptop. I had it serviced so I could sell it. The thought popped into my head: why don't I offer it to my mate – free of charge – as a gift. I did. He accepted (fast) and picked it up within 24 hours. Cue the dopamine explosion!

SO CONSIDER:

WHO NEEDS YOUR HELP RIGHT NOW?

Emotion

Meaning

Living with purpose
Gratitude & appreciation
Develop your intuition

Mood

Managing self-talk
Managing emotions
Managing mood

Connect

Meaningful relationships
Kindness & compassion
Connection to nature

MEANING

LIVING WITH PURPOSE
·
GRATITUDE & APPRECIATION
·
DEVELOP YOUR INTUITION

Living with purpose

> "The best way to lengthen out our days is to walk steadily and with a purpose."
>
> **Charles Dickens**

Having a strong reason to do things is important, and approaching life with purpose is widely accepted as being a vital way to achieve this. In our experience, it is also highly motivating and energizing too. So how and why does this work?

Most humans are habituated to experience a constant emotional state of mild dissatisfaction due to a natural negative bias in our brains which has been cultivated in modern education systems. **The majority of us are programmed to search for 'what is missing' or 'what is wrong',** and this has only been magnified by advertising and social media. Society makes it very hard to avoid comparing yourself to others; it stimulates you to search for 'things' or 'experiences' that promise to make you feel better. **This makes being 'happy' and contented a real challenge, and for a large number of people, practically impossible.** In fact, the odds of being contented with what we have are really stacked against us, as we're also led to believe that 'nothing is ever perfect', which keeps us trapped in this mindset. No wonder we struggle!

The good news is that there are some practical ways we can side-step this trap and find genuine fulfilment, motivation and energy to sustain ourselves over the long-term, regardless of our circumstances. And **the secret is to look for meaning instead of chasing happiness.** This is because happiness is more fleeting, whereas meaning can endure and get us through the challenges that life will throw at us. It can keep us positive even when things are tough. By understanding meaning, we can be more focused and reassured regardless of the circumstances.

+ReCharge!

So how do you do it?

The first step is to recognize what meaning is and that we can find it in many things. But what exactly is meaning?

Meaning is a way of framing something which gives whatever you are doing a sense of significance. In other words, there's a bigger purpose at play. This is why two people can do the same task – one can find meaning in it, but the other finds none!

Meaning allows us to attach a sense of significance to anything. It makes us feel good about ourselves. For some, this is looking after children, being kind, helping others, building a business or growing vegetables. It doesn't really matter what 'it' is – what is important is that it gives you a sense of meaning. We have already seen what can be achieved by FINDING JOY & SHARING; the next thing to do is to start identifying all the ways you find meaning and then build a strategy to experience more of them regularly in your life.

So reflect on the questions on the next page and notice during the next week what are some of the things that give you the deepest satisfaction and meaning. By reflecting on why, it will allow you to create a deeper sense of meaning.

> "He who has a why to live can bear almost any how."
>
> **Friedrich Nietzsche**

Living with purpose

Here are mine:

What gives me meaning	Why it gives me meaning
Time with my daughter Imogen	Makes me feel like I'm investing in my future, passing on my learning while getting a tonne of life-lessons too! Plus – she's a hoot.
Coaching clients	Helping others makes me feel valuable, and that I'm contributing to making people's lives better
Connecting conversations with close friends	Helps me make sense of my journey and keeps me grateful for the support and love I get

TO EXPLORE LIVING WITH PURPOSE FURTHER, HERE ARE TWO FURTHER RESOURCES FOR YOU:

Ikigai: The Japanese Secret to a Long and Happy Life by Albert Liebermann and Hector Garcia

Man's Search for Meaning by Victor E. Frankl

+ReCharge!

We will now explore the other elements of MEANING – GRATITUDE AND APPRECIATION and how to DEVELOP YOUR INTUITION.

Living with purpose – Application activity

Now reflect on your areas of meaning:

What gives me meaning	Why it gives me meaning

Once you've identified them, envisage yourself doing these things. Notice the feelings you have. Realise that they are available to you at any time and consider prioritising them.

EMOTION – MEANING

Gratitude & appreciation

"When I started counting my blessings, my whole life turned around."

Willie Nelson

I thought this was a book on resilience, so why focus on gratitude and appreciation? Because it is a resilience superpower!

Here's why:

"According to the research, gratitude's psychological benefits are legion: It can lift depression, help you sleep, improve your diet, and make you more likely to exercise. Heart patients recover more quickly when they keep a gratitude journal. A recent study showed gratitude causes people to be more generous and kinder to strangers. Another study found that gratitude is the single best predictor of well-being and good relationships, beating out twenty-four other impressive traits such as hope, love, and creativity. As the Benedictine monk David Steindl-Rast (TED talk: Want to be happy? Be grateful) says, "Happiness does not lead to gratitude. Gratitude leads to happiness."" [25]

A.J. Jacobs

No surprise then that many of these benefits directly feed our resilience charge. Plus, in our experience, expressing gratitude feels great too!

+ReCharge!

Here are four practical things you can practice over the next seven days to develop gratitude and appreciation:

Gratitude & appreciation – Application activity

1. **Start cultivating the daily habit of consciously being grateful.** For the next seven days, before you start work, aim to express gratitude for at least 10 things in your life, e.g. your health, your home, your family, your wealth, your friends, your colleagues, your car, your gadgets, the food you've eaten in the last 24 hours, etc. The aim is to say it out loud, but not necessarily to another person (unless it relates to them and they are present). What if I feel grumpy and don't want to do it? Do it anyway! But I feel stressed to the eyeballs and just want the pressure to end – I don't feel grateful. Do it anyway! Notice the impact on your mood

2. **Start noticing people, both inside and outside of work, who are doing a good job**. Why? Because the act of noticing is a crucial part of cultivating gratitude; you can't be grateful if your attention is scattered

3. **Consciously practice expressing gratitude and appreciation to people every day.** Make it specific, e.g. to a team member: "I appreciated the colours you used on that spreadsheet – it made it easier for me to work with it." To the waiter at the restaurant: "Thank you for the excellent way you have taken care of us."

4. **Plan to express gratitude to all the family members in your house this coming weekend.** Consider what you have appreciated about each of them this week and express it over the weekend. Notice how it affects the mood in the family

Develop your intuition

> "The intuitive mind is a sacred gift and the rational mind is a faithful servant. We have created society that honors the servant and has forgotten the gift."
>
> **Albert Einstein**

Have you ever had the experience that as you are performing a task, you start sensing that something isn't right? Maybe it was a journey to somewhere new that wasn't going as planned, or a project at work that was about to go off-track?

That's your intuition and it is very powerful:

"Our gut intuition accesses our accumulated experiences in a synthesized way, so that we can form judgments and take action without any logical, conscious consideration... the latest findings in decision neuroscience suggest that our judgements are initiated by the unconscious weighing of emotional tags associated with our memories rather than by the conscious weighing of rational pros and cons: we start to feel something—often even before we are conscious of having thought anything."

Andrew Campbell and Jo Whitehead[26]

Furthermore, **our unconscious can process a lot more data than our conscious minds. It presents that analysis as feelings in our gut.** After our brains, our guts have more neurons (nerve fibres) than any other part of the body. That's why neuroscientists are calling it the second brain.

In analysing industrial accidents, such as the explosion on BP's Macondo oil rig in the Gulf of Mexico in 2010, there is virtually always someone involved who had a gut feeling that something wasn't right. Sadly, they often didn't do anything about it, or if they did, they weren't taken seriously. The consequences can be dire.

In the rational world of business, it is easy to discount our gut feelings about issues. With all the recent insights about unconscious bias, we are right not to trust it blindly.

+ReCharge!

That said, our gut feeling is flagging something important that we would be wise to consider, even if we decide not to act on it.

There is a part of ourselves (sometimes called the soul or spirit) that knows what is best for us. It strives for fullness of life and health. When we are thrashing ourselves way too hard and heading for burnout or self-destruction, most people get an inner sense that something is very wrong – a gut feeling or a deep inner knowing. At other times, we get an aching or yearning that we need to move on to something new. When it comes to managing our levels of resilience charge, we would be wise to listen to those yearnings and knowings.

So your gut instinct can help you make better, faster decisions, saving valuable time. **When it comes to developing your resilience, your gut instinct is good at alerting you to issues you aren't paying enough attention to, such as your wellbeing and self-care.** Cultivating a sensitivity to it is therefore extremely worthwhile.

Some practical ways to do this:

Develop your intuition – Application activity

1. Consciously pay attention to your gut instincts about situations. Start asking yourself a question: 'What's my gut telling me about this?' Write down the answer in your notebook or journal

2. Start noticing the different sensations your inner critic[45] generates, versus your sensual impulses and urges, versus your gut instinct. In which part of your body do you experience them? What is the difference between them? Can you think of a helpful metaphor to distinguish between them? Here are some examples I've used: The Tyrant, The Sugar-Seeker, and The Wise Whisperer

3. Ask yourself this question towards the end of the week: 'What's my gut telling me about how I need to care for myself this weekend?' Write down the answer in your notebook or journal. What could you do about it?

Emotion

Living with purpose
Gratitude & appreciation
Develop your intuition

Meaning

Managing self-talk
Managing emotions
Managing mood

Mood

Meaningful relationships
Kindness & compassion
Connection to nature

Connect

MOOD

MANAGING SELF-TALK

·

MANAGING EMOTIONS

·

MANAGING MOOD

Managing self-talk

"Freedom is the ability to instantly transform a bad mood into a good one."

Marty Rubin

We are all heavily influenced by our moods. They create the main themes in how we experience life. Our thoughts and feelings create emotions that flow into building mood patterns which govern our way of interacting with the world through our actions and decisions.

While we are largely unable to control this flow until moods are formed, we can influence them, and they can become a choice. But to have a choice in what constitutes our mood, we need to allow this input of thoughts, feelings and emotions to really flow through us – and this is not easy – or often intuitive.

Many of us have been brought up to repress or control this input and this has put a taboo on strong emotions like anger and sadness being acceptable. Yet the truth is that we all experience a similar range of emotions, and real freedom – and through it the choice to control our moods – is only available if we can acknowledge all our emotions and let the strong ones, particularly those that make us feel uncomfortable, flow through us.

Denying emotions doesn't really work. They might be temporarily blocked, but they will come back stronger another time, so we might as well let them flow through us. However, there is good news. All emotions – even the overwhelming strong ones – don't last for more than 90 seconds if you allow them to flow through you.[27]

+ReCharge!

This chapter will introduce you to the range of emotions and moods that you can expect to experience and will give you powerful tools to manage them. We will address MANAGING SELF-TALK, then MANAGING EMOTIONS and MANAGING MOOD.

"We all have two different voices inside us: one that is nurturing, and one that is critical; one that lifts up, and one that weighs us down. Both voices have a role to play. Our inner nurturer brings self-compassion and encouragement, while the inner critic helps you recognize where you've gone wrong and what you need to do to set things right. But for most people, the inner critic goes way overboard, throwing dart after dart of scolding, shaming, nit-picking and fault-finding. It's big and powerful, while the inner nurturer is small and ineffective, wearing down your mood, self-worth and resilience. Happily, there are good ways to reset this balance by restraining the critic and strengthening the nurturer inside yourself."

Rick Hanson PhD & Forrest Hanson[28]

"I don't want to be at the mercy of my emotions. I want to use them, to enjoy them, and to dominate them."

Oscar Wilde

Managing self-talk

'Feelings
are much
like waves,
we can't
stop them
from coming
but we can
choose which
one to surf'

Jonatan Martensson

Your self-talk plays a big role in shaping the emotions and moods that you live in. By understanding and managing your self-talk, you will have so much more energy to focus on what matters. Here are some tactics to use right now to help you start managing your inner critic:

Managing self-talk – Application activity

- ***Accept that you have one and that it's normal!*** "We've never met anyone without an inner-critic." (Halpern B, Lubar K [2003 p27] 'Leadership presence: Dramatic techniques to reach out, motivate, and inspire.')

- ***You can't change something you are not aware of, so start noticing the pattern of YOUR self-talk.*** Try writing it down in your journal. That way you can look at it and decide whether you want to listen to it. We often find that when we do this, we either feel embarrassed, because it's so untrue, or burst out laughing because it is so ridiculous! The key thing is, it has stopped having power over us

- ***Consider where it is coming from.*** Is there something familiar about the words, tone or attitude in the self-criticism? Does it remind you of anyone? Again, we have found that once we get a sense of where it's coming from, its power diminishes. It's as if we're saying, "I know you used to say that, but I'm no longer giving you the authority to speak that over me."

- Some critical self-talk doesn't come into the ridiculous category but has a grain of truth

+ReCharge!

and may even poke at a deeply held fear. In this case, you might need to do some more work and **analyse the validity of your self-talk** by asking:

o Does the evidence support the claims of your inner critic? (The inner critic tends to exaggerate, even catastrophise!)

o How balanced are the points? (The inner critic normally has an unhealthy focus on the negative or the risks)

o What is it costing me to believe it and am I happy to keep paying that cost?

o Where does this come from, and do I still give authority to that person/source?

o Having done this, we find it helpful to convert our analysis into a new dialogue – one that is more empowering. For example, I've got an important presentation coming up and the inner critic says, "You'll be boring and it's going to bomb". My re-worked self-talk (which I write down) may say, "I might be a little nervous – that's normal – but I'll be well-prepared, and I have a history of delivering engaging presentations."

"There can be no transforming of darkness into light and of apathy into movement without emotion."

Carl Gustav Jung

Managing emotions

> "One of the
> best things
> you can
> do for your
> emotional
> health is to
> beef up your
> concepts of
> emotions."
>
> **Lisa Feldman Barrett** [29]

What are emotions?

What do we mean by emotions and how are they formed?

Emotions are a chemical physiological response to a perceived presence which has been triggered by thoughts and sensations and lasts about six seconds[30]. In other words, your body senses something and produces a chemical. If you see a tiger, adrenalin is produced to signal fear. Similarly, if you see a baby, serotonin is produced to signal contentment and so on.

These 'signals' or feelings are simply how your body 'feels' emotions, such as having a tight chest, butterflies in the stomach, etc. Researchers[31] used to talk about eight basic feelings that we experience, grouped into four pairs of polar opposites:

JOY ⟷ SADNESS

ANGER ⟷ FEAR

TRUST ⟷ DISTRUST

SURPRISE ⟷ ANTICIPATION

+ReCharge!

More recently researchers[32] have expanded this list to 27:

1. Admiration
2. Adoration
3. Aesthetic Appreciation
4. Amusement
5. Anxiety
6. Awe
7. Awkwardness
8. Boredom
9. Calmness
10. Confusion
11. Craving
12. Disgust
13. Empathetic pain
14. Entrancement
15. Envy
16. Excitement
17. Fear
18. Horror
19. Interest
20. Joy
21. Nostalgia
22. Romance
23. Sadness
24. Satisfaction
25. Sexual desire
26. Sympathy
27. Triumph

> "We cannot selectively numb emotions, when we numb the painful emotions, we also numb the positive emotions."
>
> **Brene Brown**

As we saw from the tiger example, emotions are generally telling you something important – they are invaluable sources of data. To make the most of that data, ask yourself: What is it telling you? What is it trying to signal?

For example, feeling a growing sense of dissatisfaction with your work might be indicating that you're working too hard and need more joy in your life. Alternatively, it might be revealing that you are not getting as much meaning from the work you're doing, and that it could be time to consider alternatives.

Managing emotions

> "Let's not forget that the little emotions are the great captains of our lives and we obey them without realizing it."
>
> **Vincent Van Gogh**

Our emotions can also help us understand our deepest values. A situation that triggers a strong emotional reaction in you might cause little or no reaction in a colleague. This could be explained by considering whether something you value (or hate) has been activated.

We know that emotions can have a significant impact on our mental focus, our energetic state and our behaviour. They can both elevate and drain us.

Think back to a situation where you felt strong emotions, such as in a heated discussion with someone, or a piece of work you were doing that flowed unexpectedly well and led to a pleasing outcome. It will have affected you mentally, energetically and behaviourally.

Some spikes of emotions, such as anger or fear, can lead us to think and act in ways that we may regret. Part of nurturing our resilience requires us to become competent at managing some of these inevitable spikes. How?

> *"The first system we must take care of is our own."*
>
> **John Whittington**

+ReCharge!

Managing emotions –
Application activity

Step 1

You can't manage what is beyond your awareness, so step 1 is to start increasing your awareness of some of the feelings you are experiencing. How? Consciously stop and ask yourself, 'How am I feeling right now?' For instance, use going to the bathroom or getting a drink as a trigger for asking yourself this question.

You can chart your feelings by using the below model.

Inspired by the JCA Feelings Wheel [46]

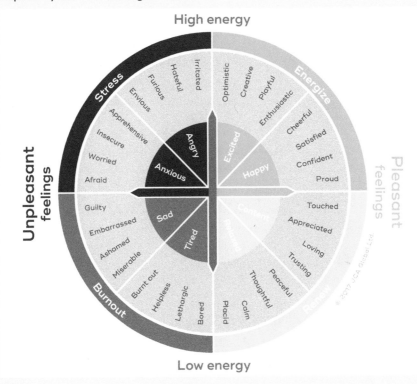

Managing emotions

> 'I want to connect my guitar to human emotions'
>
> **BB King**

Becoming more skilled at distinguishing between different feelings is a very important capability to cultivate. For example, how is overwhelm different from fatigue? Use the table at the start of this chapter as a prompt to help you to get better at distinguishing between different shades of feelings.

You may need to find a little bit of space to focus on the feeling. Try asking yourself: Where am I experiencing the sensation of it? Describe the sensation to yourself, maybe by writing in your journal.

"In a collection of scientific studies, people who could distinguish finely among their unpleasant feelings were 30 percent more flexible when regulating their emotions, less likely to drink excessively when stressed, and less likely to retaliate aggressively against someone who has hurt them."

Lisa Feldman Barrett, neuroscientist (2018)

A great follow-on question is, 'What is causing me to feel that way? What was the trigger?' Was it the way I was thinking about a situation? In this way you deepen your self-knowing, which is a precursor to self-mastery.

It's worth noting that a lot of feelings dissipate when we focus on them like this. This can reduce their grip on us. Similarly, slowing down and breathing deeply can have a similar effect.

Sometimes, talking to someone who is skilled at listening can help you deepen your understanding of your feelings. This is one of the functions performed by coaches and psychotherapists.

+ReCharge!

How does this play out, live, in a high-octane situation?

If you are live in a high-octane situation and you feel at risk of losing control and doing something you regret, apply these principles by doing the following:

1. Acknowledge how you are feeling (at the very least to yourself and possibly to the people involved)

2. Consciously slow down your breathing. In the earlier chapter on attention training we talked about either inhaling and exhaling for a count of 6. This will slow down your crazy self-talk and the emotions pumping through your chest

3. Amy Gallo[33] recognises that, 'Sitting still when you're having a difficult conversation can make the emotions build up rather than dissipate. Experts say that standing up and walking around helps to activate the thinking part of your brain.' Just be sure to let people know what you're doing or it might look a bit weird!

4. Slow down your speed of reacting to what's being said. Have you noticed how when things start getting testy, people generally talk louder and more quickly than normal and respond fast (if they even wait for the speaker to finish!). Consciously slowing down can be an effective way of regaining control; maybe even ask for or propose a break

Managing emotions – Application activity

Step 2

Consciously consider how you can recategorize how you feel by changing your self-talk about those feelings. For example, if you're about to go into an important meeting and feel your heart racing, you might categorize your sensations as harmful anxiety ("Oh no, I'm doomed!") or as helpful anticipation ("I'm energized and ready to go!").

Research[47] shows that people who recategorize anxiety as excitement enjoy positive effects and perform better in high-stress situations. These tactics work!

EMOTION – MOOD

Managing mood

> "Genius is the ability to renew one's emotions in daily experience."
>
> **Paul Cezanne**

The cocktail of emotions and feelings in your mind and body combine to produce your mood, which is a more persistent state. In other words, **emotions and feelings are more fleeting and moods last longer.**

What is a mood?

It is a state I live in and it heavily influences how I see the world. For example, an exciting but stretching opportunity presents itself; someone who lives in a mood of ambition will perceive that very differently to someone who lives in a mood of overwhelm.

It also has a huge impact on energy levels. As a leader, it is worth noting that teams, as well as individuals, live inside of moods, and these can have a significant influence on what a team believes is possible.

I may have a mood that permeates all my life; alternatively, I may live inside certain moods concerning different areas of my life, for instance my mood around my career progression, or my mood around certain relationships.

It is easier to spot other people's moods; I'm sure you can call to mind people who live in a mood of resignation, pessimism or optimism. It is much harder to spot your own mood!

Here are four moods that you will see a lot:

	I assess that:	
	I cannot change things	**I can change things**
I oppose	Resentment	Resignation
I accept	Acceptance (peace)	Ambition

+ReCharge!

Being human means that we live in a predominant mood and this manifests itself in our speech, our energy levels and our bodies. Someone in a predominant mood of ambition looks, feels and sounds very different to someone who lives in a mood of resignation. Here's how they might look:

	Mood of resignation	Mood of ambition
Self-talk:	"It'll never change, nothing will make a difference"	"I can make things happen"
Focus:	• What cannot be done • Why it cannot be done	• What do I/you/we want? • What's possible?
Actions/ Behaviours:	• Rationalising, justifying the status quo • Undermining ambitious conversations	• Generating possibilities for self and others – ongoing

Managing mood – Application activity

A critical question to ask yourself is, 'What mood do I predominantly live in?' There are two places you can usefully look:

1. The predominant content of your self-talk

2. Ask people who know you well and whose opinion you trust

To help with this question, here is a longer list of different moods:

Unpleasant Moods	Pleasant Moods
• Resentment	• Wonder
• Despair	• Ambition
• Confusion	• Sincerity
• Resignation	• Confidence
• Panic	• Acceptance
• Arrogance	• Trust
• Overwhelm	• Curiosity

Managing mood

> "If your emotional abilities aren't in hand, if you don't have self-awareness, if you are not able to manage your distressing emotions, if you can't have empathy and have effective relationships, then no matter how smart you are, you are not going to get very far."
>
> **Daniel Goleman**

Is it possible to shift your mood?

Yes!

But it may not be easy – because they take root in:

- Our patterns of self-talk, which create grooves that can be hard to break
- The way we see ourselves
- The way we physically hold ourselves all of which has influences
- The way others see us

How do you shift your mood?

Follow these four steps:

#1 **Recognize the mood**

#2 **Remember – it's driven by your self-talk**

#3 **Craft some different self-talk concerning the future**

#4 **Commit to new actions that support the new self-talk**

+ReCharge!

Managing mood – Application activity

1. Work out the predominant moods that you live in

2. Start noticing and naming to yourself the predominant moods of people around you

3. If you have a predominant mood that doesn't serve you, practice shifting it using the four steps opposite.

"The truly free individual is free only to the extent of her own self-mastery... those who will not govern themselves are condemned to find Masters to govern them."

Stephen Pressfield

Emotion

Meaning

Living with purpose
Gratitude & appreciation
Develop your intuition

Mood

Managing self-talk
Managing emotions
Managing mood

Connect

Meaningful relationships
Kindness & compassion
Connection to nature

CONNECT

MEANINGFUL RELATIONSHIPS
·
KINDNESS & COMPASSION
·
CONNECTION TO NATURE

Meaningful relationships

> "Our
> connections
> to all the
> things
> around
> you literally
> define who
> you are."
>
> **Aaron D. O'Connell**

One of the most remarkable things about human relationships is our ability to inspire, energize and elevate others. It truly is one of the most beautiful gifts of being human, and at its essence is connection.

When we are able to connect in an authentic way, without pretence or performance, a lot of real magic happens. We become more energized and resilient, we get to know ourselves better in relationship with others, and we become more truthful to ourselves and others.

The pressure of pretence, in other words the tendency to keep relating to others in a superficial, courteous and pleasing way, can be overwhelming and draining. And while it has an occasional use in being civil and polite, it is something that has become over-conditioned into many of us from an early age. If we are unable to pierce this superficiality, then our capacity to resolve our issues and deal with negative self-talk also diminishes. Conversely, when we are able to penetrate beneath the surface, we can be comforted, reassured and energized in powerful ways.

The rest of this final chapter will look at how we build this connection with others, through KINDNESS AND COMPASSION and will also look at how we can deepen this within ourselves through our CONNECTION TO NATURE.

Feeling a deep connection to others is a primal need for most people. And perhaps the greatest source of joy in our lives comes from our relationships. Yet, **in the busyness of our lives, it's easy to forget to cultivate the relationships that can nourish us.** The good news is that we don't need many relationships, but the quality of the few we have can really elevate us and make a huge difference to our wellbeing.

In this section we'll share some reflections on how to cultivate those relationships.

+ReCharge!

"Healthy relationships are a vital component of health and wellbeing. There is compelling evidence that strong relationships contribute to a long, healthy, and happy life. Conversely, the health risks from being alone or isolated in one's life are comparable to the risks associated with cigarette smoking, blood pressure, and obesity."

Mary Jo Kreitzer, RN, PhD[34]

From a resilience perspective, being a lone ranger is high risk. Being distanced from any meaningful and messy contact with others might leave you feeling safe and cosy, but research shows that you are in fact vulnerable.

Scientifically validated research, referenced in the source above, shows that healthy relationships can help you live longer, deal with stress better, be healthier and feel richer. On the other hand, low social support is linked to several health consequences, such as depression, decreased immune functions and higher blood pressure. This is a BIG deal for managing your energy.

Furthermore, maintaining a pretence of <insert your favourite trait, e.g. coping> is tiring; it's a waste of energy. This is why in all our programmes we place an emphasis on building authentic vulnerable relationships in a small group setting.

"We are like islands in the sea, separate on the surface but connected in the deep."

William James

Meaningful relationships

> "Friendship is born at that moment when one person says to another: 'What! You too? I thought I was the only one."
>
> **C.S. Lewis**

There are some significant challenges with building authentic relationships in a corporate context: corporates are incredibly busy and value strength and uninterrupted flow. There often isn't the space to be real. It can also feel and be risky to be open about how you are really doing – people may not know how to respond, or they may exploit what you have revealed.

Despite this tension, we can experience significant value when it happens. For example, we led two different twelve-month programmes for people at the senior levels of two large professional service firms – seriously bright and high-earning executives. In both programmes, it was the monthly two-hour small group meetings that people said most helped them to change. When asked why, we received comments like:

- "It was so nice to know that my colleague, who seems so slick and confident, was struggling with the same issues as me – it helped me to keep going with trying to change."

- "It's the first time I've experienced community at work and it's a drug I want more of – so nourishing and energizing."

It's surprisingly energizing to take the power out of those stories we run in our minds, e.g. "such and such a colleague never struggles and is simply brilliant." Suddenly, we are not alone.

Weblink, scan the code.

Scan the code for a TED article: How to build closer relationships

+ReCharge!

Here are some ways to allow more meaningful relationships to develop:

1. **Practise responsible vulnerability –** sharing what's going on in your internal world, especially when everything isn't as you'd want it to be. Experiment with being gradually, but increasingly, more real and open with people and see what the impact is. For example, last week, I'd sent a fee proposal to a client and I'd not heard a peep from them. My catastrophising self-talk was in overdrive. I shared this with a group I was working with. I was surprised how my perspective shifted and how much better I felt about it!

2. **Practise giving people your full attention.** Acknowledge any internal self-talk that's triggered as you chat and choose to let it go; focus instead on their face, body, emotions and what they are saying. Try and name the emotion they are expressing, e.g. "I can see you are feeling quite <troubled/excited/relieved> by this situation."

3. Choose to be big and **step over any previous offence or hurt** that someone has caused you. Why? "Sometimes in life, it's not until the worst happens – death, illness, divorce, job loss – that we make it a priority to reassess our relationships, to cultivate the ones we already have and to mend ones that have been broken." (Wellness Specialist Elizabeth Lesser). Why wait for the crisis?! Is there anyone you need to build bridges with? What might the next step be?

4. **Plan to spend time with people whose company you enjoy** and who nourish you. Plan different ways to have fun! Recently, I spent half a day off-road biking at Cannock Chase, in Staffordshire in the UK, with two of my adult kids. We got plastered in mud, shed a little bit of blood (pedal on shin wound!) and had an enormous piece of cake afterwards. We are still talking about it!

Meaningful relationships – Application activity

Choose one person or situation you would like to develop more openness with and visualise yourself practicing ways of being more intentional about making that happen.

Kindness & compassion

> "Be kind, for everyone you meet is fighting a harder battle."

Plato

There are certain qualities which help to connect us to others, while at the same time giving us energy and boosting our resilience. Kindness and compassion are two of those qualities. So why focus on them, and in particular, self-compassion?

Because:

"Psychologists are discovering that self-compassion is a useful tool for enhancing performance in a variety of settings, from healthy aging to athletics. I and other researchers have begun focusing on how self-compassion also enhances professional growth. When people treat themselves with compassion, they are better able to arrive at realistic self-appraisals, which is the foundation for improvement. They are also more motivated to work on their weaknesses rather than think "What's the point?" and to summon the grit required to enhance skills and change bad habits. Self-compassion does more than help people recover from failure or setbacks. It also supports what Carol Dweck, a psychology professor at Stanford University, has called a 'growth mindset.'"

Serena Chen[35]

We know that many of these benefits directly feed our resilience charge.

+ReCharge!

What is self-compassion?

Self-compassion means resisting the urge to harshly judge yourself or others, particularly when things haven't gone as well as you hoped for. Instead, it creates a sense of self-worth, because it leads people to genuinely care about their own well-being and recovery after a setback. You can probably see the link between this definition and the section in MOOD – MANAGING SELF-TALK on handling the inner critic (who doesn't do self-compassion!).

Here are some practical questions you can ask yourself to cultivate self-compassion, particularly after a situation you found difficult:

> "Love and compassion are necessities, not luxuries. Without them, humanity cannot survive."
>
> **Dalai Lama XIV,**
> *The Art of Happiness*

Kindness & compassion – Application activity

1. Am I being kind and understanding to myself?

2. Do I acknowledge shortcomings and failure as experiences shared by everyone?

3. Am I keeping my negative feelings in perspective?

4. If this doesn't work, a simple "trick" can also help: Sit down and write yourself a letter in the third person, as if you were a friend or loved one. Many of us are better at being a good friend to other people than to ourselves, so this can help avoid spirals of defensiveness or self-flagellation

Kindness & Compassion

> "I've been searching for ways to heal myself, and I've found that kindness is the best way."
>
> **Lady Gaga**

What is compassion?

Compassion literally means "to suffer together." Among emotion researchers, it is defined as the feeling that arises when you are confronted with another's suffering and feel motivated to relieve that suffering.

Greater Good magazine[36]

How on earth is engaging in another's suffering good for my resilience?

Research has shown that when we feel compassion, our heart rate slows down, we secrete the "bonding hormone" oxytocin, and regions of the brain linked to empathy, caregiving, and feelings of pleasure light up, which often results in our wanting to approach and care for other people.

Greater Good magazine[37]

In manageable quantities, compassion is good for us and it deepens our relationships.

In corporate life, BMW (Blaming, Moaning and Whining) conversations take up a lot of energy. Take these examples:

- 'You'll never guess what she did?'
- 'He said this about me in the LT (Leadership Team) meeting according to one of my sources.'

+ReCharge!

When situations like this arise, compassion is a choice, an option:

Something happens → **Strong emotions are triggered in you**

Judge, criticize, assume the worst about the other's intentions

Respond with compassion, e.g. 'There must be a good reason why they did this. I'll talk to them at the first opportunity".

As we saw in the section on sharing, **kindness towards others not only helps the recipient, but it has a neurological kick-back for us.** Furthermore, acts of kindness and compassion fuel meaningful relationships and are worth practicing.

Kindness & Compassion – Application activity

Imagine how you would feel if there was a small gift outside your front door with a note: 'I thought this might help.' After feeling bewildered for a few seconds you would probably be filled with gratitude and awe. Now, think of a small, random act of kindness you can gift to someone and plan it. Feels good, doesn't it!

Connection to nature

> "If you go off into a far, far forest and get very quiet, you'll come to understand that you're connected with everything."
>
> **Alan Watts**

One of the most powerful ways we can connect to ourselves is through being in nature. There is a considerable body of evidence to support the healing properties of being out in it. Not only does it affect everything from our mood to how our bodies heal, it also allows us to get more in the present moment and have a rest from being distracted by the stress of our busy schedules. Considering the amount of screen time that most of us now have in our lives, **there's never been a better time to discover how nature can be the antidote to the digital stress of the modern world.**

I'm very fortunate to live in Oslo, and the Nordic approach to outdoor living – or *friluftsliv* – is something of a birthright. A remarkable quality of Scandinavians is their appreciation of nature and enthusiasm to get outdoors, in any weather. The Nordic people understand the powerful reasons and the health benefits behind this approach to life, even in their cities. Opposite are some guidelines to develop more *friluftsliv* in your life and reap the benefits. And remember, just 20 minutes outside is enough to boost your mental sharpness and reduce your blood pressure – and best of all it's free. Plus, it is possible in any setting, whether a suburb or the centre of a busy metropolis.

+ReCharge!

Here are some ways you can start discovering nature's benefits in your life:

Connection to nature – Application activity

1. Plan a 20-minute walk alone during or after your work schedule next week in your nearest park

2. Plan a short excursion with your family to the nearest nature reserve to discover what lives there

3. Plan a trip to the nearest source of water (river, stream, lake, beach) and take in the energy you get from it

4. Notice how you think and feel afterwards

And finally...

5. Consider a challenge you have that would benefit from getting a different perspective and repeat #1 to experience it.

> "Look deep into nature, and then you will understand everything better."
>
> **Albert Einstein**

"TAKE CARE OF YOUR EMPLOYEES AND THEY WILL TAKE CARE OF YOUR BUSINESS."

RICHARD BRANSON

How leaders can build the resilience of their teams

> "If we cannot disconnect, we cannot lead. Creating the culture of burnout is opposite to creating a culture of sustainable creativity... This mentality needs to be introduced as a leadership and performance-enhancing tool."
>
> **Arianna Huffington**

As a leader, you have three responsibilities towards your people regarding their energetic wellbeing (resilience):

1. You are a role model! Like it or not, people are looking at you (consciously or unconsciously). They are taking their lead from you concerning whether it is OK to manage their resilience in this team

2. You are in position of authority which you can use to proactively look out for the energetic wellbeing (resilience) of your team members

3. You are in a position of authority, which you can use to set the team's ways of working which can support everyone's energetic wellbeing (resilience)

Let's look at each of these briefly:

+ReCharge!

You are a role model

Even though your organisation has both an aspirational culture as well as the one that operates in reality, each team has its own microculture. According to research by Performance Climate Systems,[38] 70% of that is shaped by the leader – you! Your team are unconsciously taking their lead from you. For example:

- If you're late for meetings, that sends a message that it's OK for them to be late for them

- If you play a bit fast and loose with expenses, they may follow suit

- If you're a committed learner and keep up to date on trends and disruption affecting your profession and sector, it'll probably rub off on your team

When they look at how you consciously manage your energy levels, what do they see? For example:

1. Is it OK to block out distractions, or not respond immediately to emails and messages, in order to focus on an important piece of work and create the conditions for flow to happen?

2. Is it OK to have boundaries between work and important things outside of work? Is it OK to challenge people who violate those boundaries?

3. To what extent is it OK to prioritize appropriate self-care?

4. To what extent is it OK to say you're struggling with an issue?

5. To what extent do team members look out for each other and raise concerns if someone is thrashing themselves?

6. Is it OK to switch off your work phone and not respond to work emails in the evening and at weekends?

7. Do you express appreciation to people?

8. Despite all the imperfections of your organisation, do you express gratitude for what is working and going well?

9. Is it OK to speak up, raise questions and share perceptions based on intuition and a felt sense of something?

How leaders can build the resilience of their teams

> "Remember teamwork begins by building trust. And the only way to do that is to overcome our need for invulnerability."

Patrick Lencioni

10. Are you emotionally safe? Do your emotions and mood cast a long shadow over the team?

11. Is it OK to be appropriately vulnerable or do I have to present as being in control?

How leaders can build the resilience of their teams – Application activity

Take some time to ponder these questions, and then consider asking your team members these questions – maybe one or two to each person. Be sure to set a good context before asking the questions, for example by saying that you are concerned about the example you are setting regarding self-care and energy management, and that you'd like to test out perceptions.

+ReCharge!

Looking out for the energetic wellbeing (resilience) of your team members

How to spot resilience issues with team members – the signs.

There are a number of indicators of a team member's energetic wellbeing (resilience):

1. As a leader you will have a felt sense of how each person in your team is doing. Whilst this isn't 'the truth', it is an extremely valuable source of data for all the reasons explained in the chapter on MEANING

2. Any changes in their energy and mood that you observe or sense. Take a look at the emotion wheel in the MOOD chapter and ask yourself where a team member seems to be most of the time. Are they behaving as they normally would? Perhaps they seem out of sorts? More agitated or withdrawn? Or they're just not themselves

3. Any changes in their level of productivity

4. Any changes in their physical appearance

If you sense something isn't right, trust that gut instinct and act on it. Here's how to do it:

> "Employees who said they completely trust their team leader were 14 times more likely to be fully engaged. Those lucky enough to completely trust their colleagues, team leader, and senior leaders, were 42 times more likely to be highly resilient."
>
> **ADP Research Institute (2021)**

How leaders can build the resilience of their teams

How to talk to team members about resilience concerns

In your one-to-ones and informal catch-ups with team members, you have the ideal opportunity to check out the accuracy of your perceptions regarding the points above.

Over time it can be helpful to create rituals that make it easier for team members to be open, and to build their belief that you genuinely care about them. One such ritual that can be valuable is using the emotion wheel in the MOOD chapter to do a check-in at the start of a one-to-one or informal conversation. Be sure to set a good context for why you are doing this (see below for an example).

What do you do if a team member is closed or defensive and not giving you much detail on how they are honestly doing?

And let's be real here – admitting that you are struggling can be career suicide in some organisations, so it might feel very risky to be honest about a problem.

If the person knows that your intentions for asking after them are motivated by care and concern, versus trying to exit them, it will help enormously. You may need to say that, especially if the wider organisation culture is known to be brutal.

The RU OK[39] organisation has suggested some great ways of making it easier for people to talk, for instance, to get into the conversation by asking:

- "I've noticed a few changes in what you've been saying/doing. How are things for you at the moment?"
- "I know there's been some big life changes for you recently. How are you going with that?"
- "You don't seem yourself lately – want to talk about it?"
- "Just checking in to see how you're doing?"
- "With everything that's going on, you've been on my mind lately, how are you?"
- "You've got a lot going on right now. How are you doing?

Encourage people to say more by saying something like:

- "What's been happening?"
- "Have you been feeling this way for a while?"
- "I'm here to listen if you want to talk more."

+ReCharge!

- "I'm not going to pretend I know what it's like for you, but I'm here to listen to why you feel the way you do."
- "It sounds like that would be really tough. How are you going with managing it?"
- "Do you feel like chatting a bit longer? I'm ready to listen."
- "So, what was that like?"
- "That's tough. Keep talking, I'm listening."
- "What you're going through isn't easy, It's good we can talk about it."
- "Thank you for sharing this with me. That can't have been easy for you."
- "Take your time, I'm here for you."
- "If there's something you're unsure about sharing with me right now, I just want you to know I'm here when you're ready?"

In terms of thinking about taking action (if it's needed) you could say:

- "What do you think is a first step that would help you through this?"
- "What can I do right now to support you?"
- "Have you spoken to your doctor or another health professional about this? It might be a matter of finding the right fit with someone."
- "Have you had much support around you?"
- "What's something you enjoy doing? Making time for that can really help."
- "Do you think it would help for you to talk to someone else about some of these things, maybe a health professional?"
- "Is there anything you've tried in the past when you've felt like this, that's made you feel better?"
- "I know when I went through something similar, talking to a professional really helped me out. Would you like me to help you book an appointment?"

All of this strongly communicates that you care for the team member. Feeling cared for can have a surprisingly positive impact on someone's motivation and performance.[40]

How leaders can build the resilience of their teams

> "It is literally true that you can succeed best and quickest by helping others to succeed."
>
> **Napolean Hill**

You are in position of authority, which you can use to set the team's ways of working

Changing anything is always easier with others. You just need to consider the power of a group dynamic, for instance Weight Watchers, to be reminded how successful this can be. The same is true with building team practices which support energetic wellbeing (resilience).

An audit team at the Big 4 audit practice Ernst & Young (EY) experimented with this at their most ferocious time of year – the audit 'busy season'. The results were surprising.[41]

The team agreed five daily practices:

1. Do your most important work when you first get to the office, for an uninterrupted stretch of 60 to 90 minutes, and then take a renewal break. Mark Twain famously said that if the first thing you do in the morning is to eat a live frog, you can go through the rest of the day knowing the worst is behind you. Your frog is your worst task, and you should do it first thing in the morning

2. Get up from your desk at lunchtime for at least 30 minutes and do some type of movement

3. After 90 minutes of work, take a break of at least five minutes. If that isn't possible, do one minute of deep breathing to clear your bloodstream of stress hormones

4. When you stop working for the day, do something that allows you to transition mentally and emotionally between work and home

5. Set a pre-sleep routine and a bedtime that ensures you get at least seven hours of sleep

+ReCharge!

Did it work?

The team's lead partner said: "It showed us the extraordinary value of intentionally taking care of ourselves."

In the five months after busy season, when accounting teams industry-wide often lose multiple team members to exhaustion and burnout, this team's retention level stood at 97.5%.

Over to you.

How leaders can build the resilience of their teams – Application activity

What practices from this book could you experiment with your team?

Here is some guidance:

1. Start small

2. Discuss and agree the experiment as a team

3. Agree how long you'll run it for

4. Agree how you'll support yourselves to see it through

5. Agree how you'll measure the impact

6. Agree how and when you'll review interim progress.

You may want to consider running our resilience programme for your entire team. We have run this with several teams and each time it has delivered impressive changes. This is partly because, when a group learns and grows together, it has far more impact than purely solo efforts. Check it out here:

https://www.rechargeability.com/corporate-program-architecture/

In closing, do all of this and you'll be surprised at the positive impact it will have on the atmosphere in your team (and its performance).

Conclusion

"It is really wonderful how much resilience there is in human nature. Let any obstructing cause, no matter what, be removed in any way, even by death, and we fly back to first principles of hope and enjoyment."

Bram Stoker, *Dracula*

One of the unseen benefits of the pandemic has been how many people have had a chance to re-assess what's important to them. Our normal routines disappeared and were replaced with something different. More challenging probably but the disruption to our normal flow has certainly given us a chance to re-set.

If you've engaged with this book in any way - then you've realised how important it is to prioritise yourself. We believe this is the best investment you can make. Not only to yourself but to those around you.

If you're serious about continuing to look after yourself and managing your energy then we would encourage you to share your experience with others.

In our experience this is the best way of deepening learning and keeping habits that will sustain you. To help with this – we would encourage you and your teams to re-take the diagnostic on a regular basis. You decide what regular means but as a minimum at least once a year.

+ReCharge!

We would also like to hear from you, so please join our Recharge community (you can sign-up here: https://www.rechargeability.com/) and share your experience with others. Your story and example might be exactly what someone else needed to read to be inspired to make the changes they needed, so please share your successes. We also welcome your feedback on any topic so please let us know what you think. And if you come across some great tips or approaches that we can use – then we will happily try them out for ourselves and who knows, possibly include them into the next version of Recharge [with a huge thank you to you!]

> "If you want to lift yourself up, lift up someone else."
>
> **Booker T. Washington**

Weblink, scan the code.

Scan the code to sign-up to the Recharge community

Endnotes

1 Sunday Times, 8 Oct 2018: Interview: Antonio Horta-Osorio: my rocky ride in the saddle at Lloyds

2 https://www.ted.com/talks/amishi_jha_how_to_tame_your_wandering_mind?language=en#t-422

3 E.g. Megan Reitz and Michael Chaskalson, 'Mindfulness Works but Only If You Work at It', Harvard Business Review, 4 Nov 2016

4 Source: "How to feel good in 10 minutes" Saturday September 12 2020, Rachel Carlyle The Times

5 https://www.successconsciousness.com/blog/letting-go/what-does-emotional-attachment-mean/ accessed on 14 May 2020

6 https://www.psychologytoday.com/gb/blog/stronger-the-broken-places/201404/what-s-wrong-being-right accessed on 14 May 2020

7 This approach comes from the work of Kegan R & Lahey L (2009) 'Immunity to change: How to Overcome It and Unlock the Potential in Yourself and Your Organization.' Harvard Business School Press, Boston MA

8 Source: https://www.sleepfoundation.org/nutrition/food-and-drink-promote-good-nights-sleep

9 Source: https://www.theguardian.com/football/2018/jul/05/england-gareth-southgate-penalties-overcome-hoodoo accessed on 26.5.20

10 Source: 'Breathing through lockdown' by Michael Cahill (2020) accessed on 26.5.20 from https://coaching-constellations.mn.co/posts/breathing-through-lockdown

11 https://www.youtube.com/watch?v=sKmKKCdnJ4U

12 Megan Reitz and Michael Chaskalson, 'Mindfulness Works but Only If You Work at It', Harvard Business Review, 4 Nov 2016

13 https://www.shrm.org/hr-today/news/hr-news/pages/turnofftech.aspx accessed on 26.5.20

14 Ibid

15 Drawing on the work of Art Markman in https://hbr.org/2017/08/how-to-forget-about-work-when-youre-not-working. August 25, 2017

16 Source: Your Life: A Practical Guide to Happiness Peace and Fulfilment

17 Neuroscientist Wendy Suzuki. TED talk: The brain-changing benefits of exercise. https://www.ted.com/talks/wendy_suzuki_the_brain_changing_benefits_of_exercise

18 Rosie Taylor in The Times, in 'Sitting at desk for 9 hours a day raises risk of early death.' 22 August 2019

19 Neuroscientist Wendy Suzuki. TED talk: The brain-changing benefits of exercise. https://www.ted.com/talks/wendy_suzuki_the_brain_changing_benefits_of_exercise

20 Rosie Taylor in The Times, in 'Sitting at desk for 9 hours a day raises risk of early death.' 22 August 2019

21 Source: https://www.webmd.com/depression/what-is-anhedonia

22 https://discpersonalitytesting.com/free-disc-test/

23 Source: https://www.takingcharge.csh.umn.edu/why-personal-relationships-are-important

24 E.g. How to be Happy: Lessons from Making Slough Happy BBC 2005

25 Source: https://ideas.ted.com/why-you-should-always-thank-your-barista/]

26 Source: 'How to test your decision-making instincts', by Andrew Campbell and Jo Whitehead in McKinsey Quarterly May 2010

27 Source: https://care-clinics.com/did-you-know-that-most-emotions-last-90-seconds/#:~:text=Menu-,Did%20you%20know%20that%20most%20emotions%20last%2090%20seconds%3F,can%20last%20a%-20long%20time!

+ReCharge!

28 Source: https://ideas.ted.com/how-to-stand-up-to-your-inner-critic/

29 Source: "Try these two smart techniques to help you master your emotions." Jun 21, 2018 / Lisa Feldman Barrett

30 Source: https://www.6seconds.org/2017/05/15/emotion-feeling-mood/

31 Robert Plutchik 1980

32 Proceedings of National Academy of Sciences, was led by Alan S. Cowen and Dacher Keltner PhD from the University of California, Berkeley (2017)

33 'How to Control Your Emotions During a Difficult Conversation,' by Amy Gallo, HBR, December 01, 2017

34 Source: https://www.takingcharge.csh.umn.edu/why-personal-relationships-are-important

35 Source: Give Yourself a Break: The Power of Self-Compassion by Serena Chen in HBR September–October 2018

36 Source: https://greatergood.berkeley.edu/topic/compassion/definition

37 Source: https://greatergood.berkeley.edu/topic/compassion/definition

38 https://www.performanceclimatesystem.com/research/ accessed on 12.10.2020

39 https://www.ruok.org.au/how-to-ask

40 Source: Buckingham M & Coffman C (1999) 'First break all the rules: What the world's greatest managers do differently.' Based on Gallup data from 105,000 employees in 2,500 business units

41 Source: What Happens When Teams Fight Burnout Together by Tony Schwartz, Rene Polizzi, Kelly Gruber, and Emily Pines. HBR. September 30, 2019

42 Megan Reitz and Michael Chaskalson, ibid

43 Taken from Boud D and Walker D, Ch 5 'Barriers to reflection on experience' in Boud D, Keogh R and Walker D (Eds) (1993) 'Using experience for learning' SRHE & Open University Press, Buckingham

44 If you are struggling to articulate how you felt, use the JCA feelings wheel, accessible at https://www.jcaglobal.com/blog/developing-resilient-leadership-get-out-of-your-head/attachment/jca-feelings-wheel/

45 See next section on EMOTION – MOOD and Managing self-talk for more information on the inner-critic

46 https://www.jcaglobal.com/mediatogotolive/wp-content/uploads/2017/12/JCA-Feelings-wheel.pdf

47 "How Emotions Are Made: The Secret Life of the Brain" by Lisa Feldman Barrett. 2017 Houghton Mifflin Harcourt Publishing Company

About the authors

Tim Farish   Matthew Gregory

Tim & Matt have been helping organizations and professionals develop globally for over forty years. Matt is based in the UK and previously worked at KPMG before setting up his own consultancy in 2007. Tim is based in Scandinavia and worked in media before going into consultancy in 2001. They met studying an MSc in Change at University of Surrey in 2002 and have been collaborating ever since. They have been living, coaching and developing the Recharge! model together since 2016.

CPSIA information can be obtained
at www.ICGtesting.com
Printed in the USA
LVHW070133280421
685801LV00019B/2066